ELEANOR OF CASTILE

By the same Author:

Olton Heritage, Brewin Books 1986
(with Margaret Jordan and Carol Andrews)

Eleanor of Castile

by
Jean Powrie

BREWIN BOOKS

First published November 1990 by
Brewin Books, Studley, Warwickshire. B80 7LG

© Jean Powrie 1990

All rights reserved

ISBN 0 947731 79 2

Typeset in Baskerville 11pt.
and made and printed in Great Britain by
Supaprint (Redditch)Ltd., Redditch, Worcs. B97 6BZ

DEDICATION

To all the 'Friends of Eleanor'

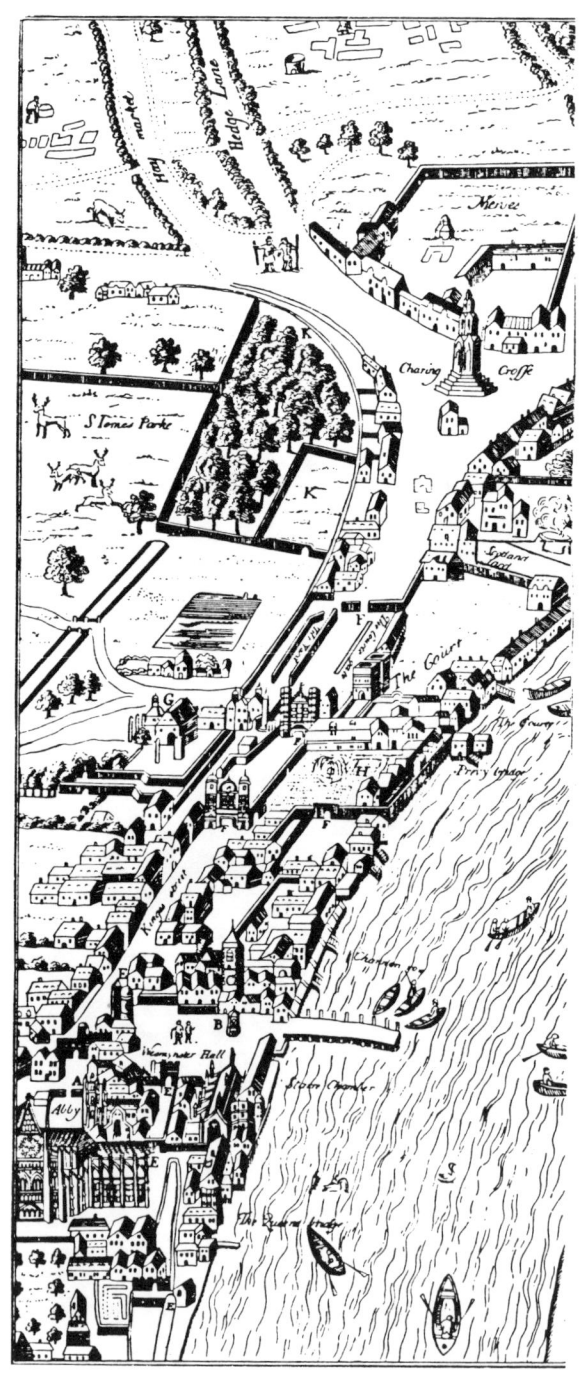

CONTENTS

		Page
Part I	Eleanor & Edward	1
Part II	The Journey to Westminster	26
Part III	Grantham	68
Part IV	Stamford	82
Part V	Geddington	100
Part VI	Northampton	109
Part VII	Stoney Stratford, Woburn, Toddington & Dunstable	128
Part VIII	St. Alban's	137
Part IX	Waltham	145
Part X	London	154
Part XI	London to Westminster	169
Part XII	Westminster	182

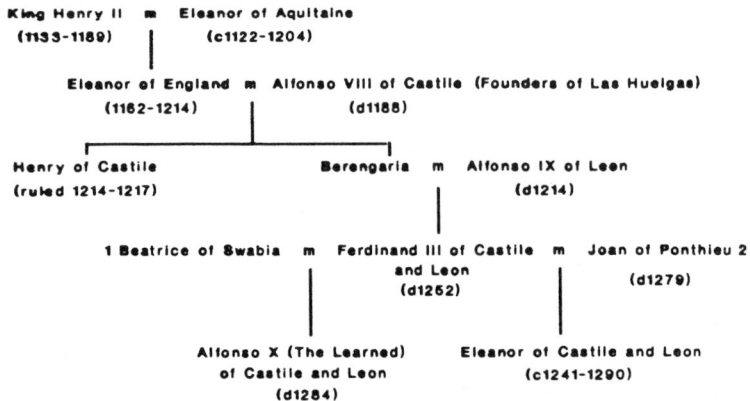

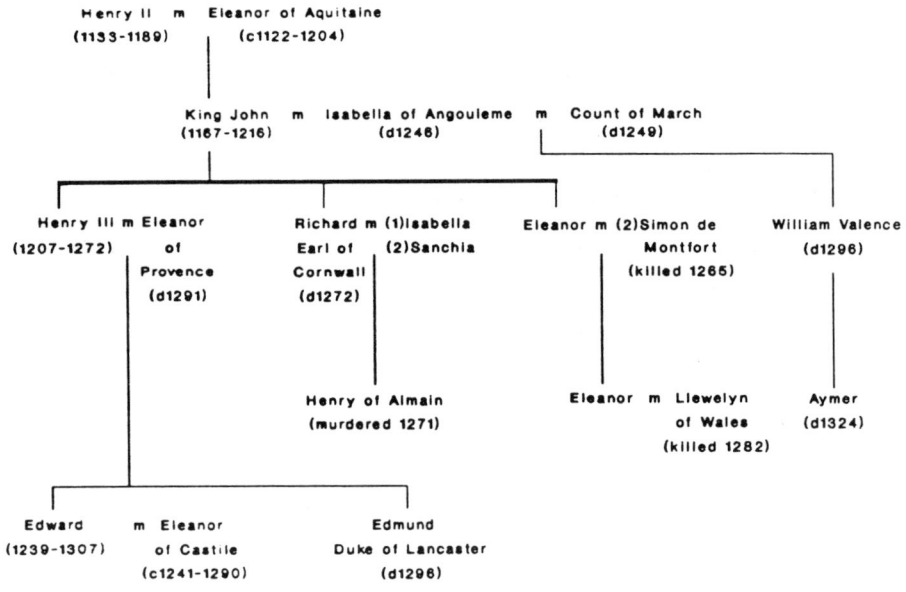

1. Eleanor & Edward.
Family Trees

PART I

Eleanor & Edward

Eleanor, the daughter of Ferdinand III of Castile and his second wife, Joan of Ponthieu, entered English history in 1253/4 on her betrothal and marriage to Edward, the son and heir of the English king, Henry III. Castile is now part of Spain, and Ponthieu, a vassal state situated on either side of the Somme estuary, was eventually absorbed into France.

Edward and Eleanor were both descended from Henry II of England (*see fig.1*). There had been a family connection of a different nature. Edward's father had been betrothed to Eleanor's mother.

Identifying the Eleanors

To differentiate Eleanor from other medieval Queen Eleanors, she is known in history as Eleanor of Castile. Her mother-in-law, Henry III's queen, is identified as Eleanor of Provence and her more famous ancestress, the wife of Henry II, as Eleanor of Aquitaine. Henry II's daughter, who married a king of Castile, is known as Eleanor of England.

Marriage

The marriage of Edward and Eleanor of Castile was the result of an agreement made between Edward's father and Eleanor's half brother, Alfonso the Learned, who was then King of Castile, Ferdinand III having died in 1252. Alfonso stipulated that the marriage was to take place 'five weeks before Michaelmas (August 25th. 1254). By the contract, Eleanor was to receive, among other things, the English villes and castles of Grantham and Stamford' and Edward, the Dukedom of Gascony together with lands in Wales. (Foedera 1253).

Initially, Henry III had endeavoured to negotiate an alliance between his son and the heiress of the Duke of Brabant, but, as Matthew Paris, a monk of St. Alban's Abbey and a chronicler of the time, wrote, Henry's ambassadors

'for some unknown reason returned sadly, with empty saddle bags, complaining their efforts and expense had been in vain.'

In August 1254 Edward would have been just 15 and Eleanor not 13 years old, but over the years they grew together and this marriage which had been politically a second best, has been idealized by chroniclers and historians as the perfect example of conjugal love.

The Castle of Burgos and Convent of Las Huelgas

Before the wedding, Edward took part in a tournament held at the Castle of Burgos. H.V. Morton, who visited the castle site in the 1950's found

'nothing to indicate where so many mighty events occurred, except a mass of weed-grown mounds and great slabs of stone, half buried in the earth.'
A large flat area, likely to have been the tilt-yard, where the jousting took place, was still discernible nearby. (Stranger in Spain).

After the tournament, Edward was knighted by Alfonso and was likely to have kept vigil (watch over his arms during the night) at the altar of the nearby convent church of Las Hueglas. This Cistercian convent had been founded by Eleanor of England and her husband, Alfonso VIII in 1170. It was here the wedding took place.

After the celebrations Edward and Eleanor crossed the Pyrenees to their Dukedom of Gascony, which had been recently ruled by Simon de Montfort, Earl of Leicester. There Edward started to learn statecraft.

England

In 1255 Eleanor came to England, accompanied by Guy de Fretun, who received 100s. expenses. Matthew Paris described her arrival at Dover, 'about the time of the feast of St. Denis' (October 9th). She came with great pomp and such a numerous retinue that her arrival

'was looked upon with suspicion by all England.'
In London there were processions, illuminations and the ringing of bells

'When she arrived at the place of her abode' Paris continues 'she found it like the dwelling of the bishop elect of Toledo - being hung with palls of silk and tapestry, like a temple - even the floor was covered with tapestry in the Spanish custom.'. . . . . 'This excessive pride excited the laughter and scorn of the English people.'

King Henry provided Eleanor with six gold-wrought cloths and six cloths of silk to offer at 'divers churches' on her journey from Dover to Westminster and a gold buckle to present at the shrine of St. Edward the Confessor in the Abbey Church of Westminster. Perhaps he sought to secure the sympathy and approval of the English Church for his daughter-in-law. It was, however, Eleanor's own character which won over the clerics and, thirty-five years later, drew from Matthew Paris's successor at St. Alban's a far kinder valediction.

Eleanor was established at Windsor Castle, where Edward had his own apartments. He joined her in November. This castle was to be their main home in England for the following nine years.

Henry and the Barons

1258-1265 was a period of conflict in England. King Henry's extravagances, his use of foreign mercenaries, promotion of his wife's European relations and dictatorial government of the country had angered the Anglo-norman barons. They found a leader in Simon de Montfort, Earl of Leicester.

The struggle was a family as well as a political one. Earl Simon was married to King Henry's sister. He had a personal grievance against Henry, as the King had not fully honoured the marriage agreement. Earl Simon was not only Edward's uncle but his godfather. At first, Edward, who sympathised with Earl Simon's ideal of a more representational government, and his cousin, Henry of Almain, supported their uncle against the King.

A temporary reconciliation, probably effected by Henry of Almain's father, 'Good' Uncle Richard (*see fig. 1*) was demonstrated at the Feast of St. Edward the Confessor (Oct. 13th.) 1260. Edward knighted Earl Simon's sons, Henry and Simon the younger, then departed for Europe. In 1261 Earl Simon also left England, Eleanor joined Edward, and King Henry was left to rule untrammelled: but the problems were merely postponed.

The Barons' War

On Christmas Eve 1262, Henry, faced with rebellion on the Welsh borders wrote to Edward, appealing for help.

'This news should bring you no joy.'
'This is no time for idleness and childishness.'
'I am getting old; you are in the flower of your youth.'
(Foedera)

Edward and Eleanor arrived in England at the end of February 1263. In April, Earl Simon returned, at the invitation of the rebel barons. Prolonged efforts to find a peaceful solution finally failed. The Feudal Host was ordered to muster at Oxford by March 30th. 1264. The rebel Barons gathered at Northampton, under the leadership of Earl Simon's sons, Henry and Simon the younger, the Earl himself being confined to his castle of Kenilworth with a broken leg.

On April 3rd. King Henry and Edward set off for Northampton. Three days later they had taken the town, possibly by the treachery of St. Andrew's Priory. The following day the Castle fell and Henry and Simon, the Earl's sons, were taken prisoners.

Earl Simon, unable to ride, was carried in a cart to London, where he had strong support amongst the Citizens. There he was joined by a powerful ally, Gilbert Clare, the young Earl of Gloucester. An attack on Rochester Castle brought Henry and Edward south. The conclusive battle of 1264 was fought at Lewes (Sussex) on May 14th.

The Battle of Lewes

Edward concentrated his attack on the London citizens. When they fled he pursued them ruthlessly. Most of the casualties were accounted Londoners. By the time Edward returned to the field the main battle was over. Uncle Richard and his son, Henry of Almain were Earl Simon's prisoners. King Henry had taken refuge in the Priory. His half-brother, William Valence and others had fled, probably hoping to join the Queen, Eleanor of Provence, in France and continue the struggle from there.

As part of the peace agreement, the Earl's sons were released, but Edward and Henry of Almain were to be his hostages. King Henry continued to rule in name, but under Earl Simon's guidance. Crown officials were replaced by the Earl's followers and the Royal Castles to be governed by Constables whom he approved.

Eleanor's Plight

During these 'disturbances in the realm' Eleanor was at Windsor, with her first child, a daughter, Katherine, probably born in March, and expecting a second child, born after December 7th, and before February 3rd. 1265: The first was the date on which £10 was allocated for a curtain, required prior to her delivery and the second when 4 marks were authorised in payment for 'cloth of murrey' lately taken in London against (in preparation for) her churching - thanksgiving for a safe delivery, strictly, celebrated forty days after the birth.

On June 16th. 1264 Earl Simon and his Council summoned the Constable, and a number of knights and their sergeants who were living at Windsor Castle, to St. Paul's to speak with the King who had 'important matters to communicate to them'. Meanwhile, the keeping of the Castle was committed to Eleanor and John de Weston, her steward - also one of the summoned knights!

The next day, King Henry, possibly as a result of this

meeting or enquiry, commanded Eleanor to leave Windsor, with her daughter, steward, Knight, household 'harness' and goods and come to Westminster and stay there and 'not to fail as the King undertakes to excuse her to Edward her lord and will keep her harmless' the latter being a promise he was not in a position to keep.

The Death of Katherine

In October, the daughter, Katherine, was dead. Moneys were allocated for cloths of gold adorned with wheels (the symbol of St. Katherine) 'for the use of Katherine, the deceased daughter of Edward, the King's first-born.'

Eleanor was in a foreign land. Her mother-in-law was in France, her father-in-law virtually a prisoner, her husband a hostage and her child dead. It would appear she had to 'borrow' money for essentials from Hugh Despenser, Simon's justiciar.

The second child was probably born at Westminster. Nothing definite is heard of it after Eleanor's churching, so it almost certainly did not survive. Dr. Parsons considers it 'may have been the Joan for whose tomb, in Westminster Abbey, Henry III ordered a gold cloth on September 7th. 1265.

Edward Escapes

Edward was moved around as a hostage, being occasionally required for official business. On April 22nd. 1265 Edward, the King, and Earl Simon were at Northampton Castle for a parliament. When Gilbert Clare, Earl of Gloucester, failed to arrive Simon realised his ally had defected. Taking Edward and Henry with him, Simon headed for Gloucester. While he parleyed with Gilbert Clare, Edward was placed in the custody of Henry de Montfort at Hereford Castle.

On May 28th. while out riding, Edward escaped with Thomas Clare, Gilbert's younger brother. They fled to Ludlow Castle, where they were joined by Roger Mortimer and Gilbert Clare. It is likely this was all part of a plot between Edward and the Clares. War was renewed.

The Battle of Evesham

On August 3rd. Earl Simon reached Evesham with King Henry. Edward arrived early the following day. In the ensuing battle, Earl Simon, his son, Henry, and Hugh Despenser all died, fighting in a circle round the King, who was wounded and rescued from the battlefield by his steward, Roger Leyburn.

After the Battle

Henry was taken to Marlborough to convalesce, but he never fully recovered. After Evesham Lord Edward, as he became, virtually ruled the Country. One of Henry's last significant acts was to deprive Earl Simon's supporters of their lands. The landless men gathered in the Isle of Axholme, while Simon Montfort the Younger's followers held out at Kenilworth Castle.

Peace

The Pope's legate, Ottoburno, with two assistants, came to England to help restore peace. All three eventually became popes - Adrian V, Gregory X and Boniface VIII. By their intercession the lands of the rebellious barons were restored on the payment of fines. The surviving children of Earl Simon, Amaury, Guy, Eleanor and Simon the younger, all left the Country. Simon de Montfort's title, Earl of Leicester, and his castle of Kenilworth were given by King Henry to his own second son, Edmund.

Domestic Matters

Edward and Eleanor's third child and first son, John, was born at Windsor in 1266, before August 23rd. when Eleanor's Thanksgiving took place at Westminster Abbey Church. This time, her mother-in-law, Queen Eleanor (of Provence), had been at Windsor to 'maintain' the household, for which she had not been reimbursed by July 3rd. 1269. John Ferre, who brought the news of John's birth to King Henry, also had to wait for his reward. However, money was instantly available for wine sent to Windsor, offerings at the shrine of St. Edward the Confessor and £7.8s.9d. for feeding the poor.

A second son, Henry, was born before May 6th.1268, when news of his birth was brought to King Henry by Aymenin, a yeoman of Eleanor. On June 1st. 1269 another of Eleanor's yeomen, John of Beaumes, brought the 'good news' of the arrival of a daughter Eleanor. The King's rewards decreased with each birth and John had an option of £10 cash or land worth at least 10 marks (£6.13s.4d.) a year.

John and Henry at Windsor

By January 1269, Windsor Castle appears to have become the establishment of John and Henry. Two tuns of Bordeaux wine and salted bucks were delivered there for 'their' use.

They grew up quickly. At the beginning of 1269, when John was not three years old and Henry not a year, they already had a tutor, a John of Reading. In 1270 Prince John was involved in a court decision, Richard Beauchamp being pardoned 'at his instance'. A licence was granted for Henry to visit France with his nurse, Joan de Somery. It is possible plans for his betrothal were already afoot. An agreement arranging the marriage of Henry with the infant Jeanne of Navarre was drawn up and dated November 3rd. 1273 (Foedera).

John received several gifts of money from his grandfather for 'his expenses'. On February 11th. 1271 the King ordered 6 dishes, 4 saucers, 2 basins, 2 goblets, and a pitcher, all of silver for his grandson. It was probably the last gift. John was dead before the end of his fifth year.

Clarendon and Guildford

With John and Henry at Windsor Castle other quarters were required for Edward and Eleanor. On December 17th. 1267 extensive alterations were ordered for the royal hunting lodge at Clarendon, near Salisbury. A long building with a pantry and buttery was to be erected for Edward and Eleanor's use. The following year 'Guildford' was also to be renovated and put at Eleanor's disposal.

Increasing Prestige

With the growth of Edward's real power and the birth of her sons, Eleanor's prestige appears to have increased. Instead of the clerk, steward, knight, ladies and domestics of Windsor (1264) she is served by The Keeper of her Wardrobe (money and treasure), The Keeper of her Chariot, Juliana de Wy, her laundress, her tailor and three clerks, William of Yatinden having been joined by John of London and Poncius de Lisle. Lisles (Insulas) had served both King John and King Henry as clerks. In 1269 two ships were to be prepared to convey Eleanor and her household 'across the sea to parts of France'. She was also granted a palfrey - the 'Rolls Royce' of horses.

Crusade 1268-1274

Lord Edward takes the Cross

While in England, the papal legate, Ottoburno, took the opportunity to preach a new crusade at St. Paul's, London, at Lincoln and at the June parliament at Northampton, where Lord Edward, his cousin Henry of Almain, and William of Valence, amongst others, 'took the cross'.

By August 1270 preparations for the crusade were complete. The government of the Country and the well-being of John, Henry and baby Eleanor were committed to Uncle Richard. Nominally, Henry III was still King. Edward and Eleanor left England.

Edward's purpose was to join his uncle, King Louis IX of France in an attack on Sultan Bibars of Egypt. However, Louis died in Tunis, before Edward's arrival. The French returned home, but Edward and Eleanor continued the crusade.

The Death of Henry of Almain

They spent the winter of 1270/1 at the court of Charles of Anjou in Sicily. Earl Simon Montfort's exiled son, Guy, had risen high in the service of Charles. Edward sent a mutual cousin, Henry of Almain, to speak with Guy. On March 13th. 1271 Guy murdered Henry while he was at Mass in a church in Viterbo, a town about 70km. north of Rome.

Acre

In 1271 Edward and Eleanor arrived at Acre, the last remaining Christian stronghold on the Syrian coast. For a while Christian militarism was revitalised by Edward's arrival and Nazareth was recaptured, but disease took its toll amongst the crusaders. A truce was proposed with Bibars which Edward refused to accept.

Attack on Edward

Edward, already sick, was brought closer to death by an attempted assassination. There are alternative accounts of this incident which differ in details but agree in essentials. They both claim Edward was stabbed by a man who had gained his confidence. Though wounded, Edward killed the attacker. The weapon had been poisoned, but Edward survived.

The story of Eleanor's saving her husband's life by sucking the poison from his wound appears later and is, therefore, usually accounted fictitious. However, there is no valid alternative and, according to the Templar's version of the attack, Eleanor was with Edward when he was roused from bed. Even if untrue, the story illustrates the growing legend of conjugal devotion.

Deaths and a Birth

Eleanor lost the child she was expecting at Acre in 1271. In England John died and King Henry wrote to Edward, begging him to return, but the following year found Edward and Eleanor still in Acre. A daughter born that year did survive. She was named Joan, probably after Eleanor's mother, and lived to marry twice, her first husband being Gilbert Clare, Earl of Gloucester. In Wales 'good' Uncle Richard died in April attacking a monastery and King Henry on November 16th. Edward was now King. The news came through Charles of Anjou.   In spite of his father's death Edward did not hurry back.

The Journey Home

He and Eleanor set off through Italy together, arriving at the papal Court on February 14th. 1273.   There Edward sought and obtained the excommunication of Guy Montfort. He then travelled to Paris, there to pay homage for his French lands to Louis' successor, Philip III.   At Chalon he took part in a tournament, probably the last time he indulged in this dangerous sport.   Eleanor visited her half-brother, Alfonso.   She then crossed the Pyrenees into Gascony, where she was joined by Edward.   It was there, on November 24th. their third son, christened Alfonso, was born.   They eventually landed in Dover on August 2nd. 1274.

Coronation

Preparations for the Coronation feast had started in February when large numbers of oxen, sheep, kids, swine, bacon pigs, rabbits, capons, hens, peacocks, cranes, and swans were ordered from sheriffs and Bishops.   On Sunday August 19th. Edward and Eleanor were jointly crowned, the first King and Queen to be so, in the new Westminster Abbey Church, which King Henry had spent 20 years building.   In subsequent documents Eleanor is referred to as the Queen Consort.   After the Coronation Feast held at Westminster Palace, 100 horses were released as gifts - for anyone who could catch them!

Death of Henry

On October 14th. less than a month after the coronation, Edward and Eleanor's son Henry died, leaving their youngest child, Alfonso, heir to the throne.

The Queen at St. Alban's

That Autumn the Queen visited St. Alban's Abbey. A dispute had arisen between the townspeople and the Abbot concerning the monopoly exercised by the Convent over the use of mills.   Rather than pay the Abbey dues, the townspeople wished to use their own mills for fulling coarse cloth and to keep handmills in their homes for grinding corn.

Hearing of the Queen's arrival, they assembled, intending to present their case.   The wily Abbot took Eleanor 'a private way' but the people 'obtained access to her'.   Eleanor censured the Abbot and questioned one of the townswomen about her grievances.   The poor woman was so overcome she could not answer, which the Abbot's chronicler reported as divine intervention! ('Deeds of the Abbots of St. Alban's Monastery').

The Birth of Margaret

In 1275 a daughter, Margaret, was born to Edward and Eleanor, the third to survive infancy. She married John - later John II Duke of Brabant, so again an alliance, thwarted in one generation, had been achieved in the next.

The Struggle with Llewelyn of Wales (1276-1277)

Llewelyn of Snowdon, Edward's vassal, had been acting independently during Edward's absence, and Edward was anxious Llewelyn should take his oath of allegiance. A document of 1276 (Close Rolls) gives Edward's account of the breakdown of the relationship. He claimed that though several venues were fixed for the renewal of Llewelyn's oath, the Prince gave 'frivolous excuses' and did not come. On the other hand, Llewelyn's proposal of the 'safe' venues of Oswestry and Montgomery argues he mistrusted Edward - a mistrust probably fostered by Edward's continuing maintenance of David, Llewelyn's treacherous brother, who had fled to England in 1274 before Edward's return. It would appear the code governing the conduct of Lords and their vassals had been violated on both sides.

Montforts Again

The situation was aggravated when, at the end of 1275, Amaury Montfort returned with his sister, Eleanor, who had been engaged to Llewelyn in the time of Earl Simon's ascendancy. Their ship was intercepted. Amaury was imprisoned and Eleanor taken to Windsor. Llewelyn's request for his fiancée's release was refused.

War

Although there was some preliminary fighting on the ever-turbulent Welsh borders, the Feudal Host was not to muster until June 26th. 1277. It would appear Edward had imposed sanctions, to reduce Llewelyn's supplies, by 1276. This, with Edward's seizure of Anglesey, the 'granary of Wales', about harvest time 1277, suggests his strategy had been, all along to isoalte Llewelyn and starve out his garrison.

During the Summer of 1277 Edward and Eleanor had been based at the Convent of Basingwerk, near the Dee Estuary. Its ruins lie about 2km. from Holywell. Founded as a house of the Order of Savigny by Ranulph, Earl of Chester in 1131, it was transferred to the Cistercians in 1147. Gerald of Wales, who visited Basingwerk in 1188, referred to it as a 'little priory'. (*see fig. 2*).

2. Basingwerk Monastery, Flintshire.

3. Rhuddlan Castle

Edward immediately set his master mason, James St. George, to build a castle, nearby. It was raised on an outcrop of rock, and became known as Flint Castle. Before it was finished James was working on a new structure close to the old Norman motte and bailey castle at Rhuddlan, on the River Clwyd. These were the first of a series of Welsh castles built by the King. (*see fig.3*).

In August, Edward and Eleanor toured Cheshire. On August 13th. they laid the foundation stone for a new abbey named Vale Royal. Eleanor left a legacy to this convent, but only £80 of it was paid (Accounts of the Queen's Executors).

It was left to her son, Edward II, to execute his 'dear mother's wishes'. (Liberate Rolls).

In September, Edward and Eleanor were back in Wales, writs being signed at the camp of 'Gannou' (Gannock i.e. Deganwy) and at Rhuddlan. From the latter, Edward ordered his Chancellor, to write to Charles of Anjou, his wife and son to let them know how he, Eleanor and their children were faring.

The Settlement with Llewelyn

Llewelyn, faced with Winter, on Snowdon, without supplies, asked for a truce. The Treaty of Conwy was drawn up. The Welsh prince came to Westminster for the Christmas Parliament and paid homage to Edward. The financial penalties which had been imposed were eased and David, Llewelyn's brother was given land in Wales.

The following year (1278) on the Day of St. Edward (October 13th.) Llewelyn and Eleanor Montfort were married at Worcester, the King and Queen being present. Amaury Montfort remained Edward's prisoner, in spite of letters from the Pope and French Court asking for his release. (Foedera).

Countess of Ponthieu

Early in 1279 Eleanor's mother, Joan of Ponthieu, died. In March, Edward was in France, negotiating with Philip III to assure Eleanor's claim to Ponthieu would be recognised, that property being, in effect, part of France. Eleanor had remained in England. On March 12th. Mary, her fourth daughter to survive, was born at Woodstock. By May, Eleanor's claim was settled. She joined Edward in France and they added Count and Countess of Ponthieu to their other titles.

The Story of Mary

A daughter born at the royal manor of Kempton in 1276 and possibly another born at Westminster in 1278 had not survived. This may have been why the next child, Mary, was 'given to God'. She was promised to Fontevrault, as a nun. This double monastery founded c.1100 was particularly associated with Eleanor of Aquitaine and Henry II of England, who, together with their son, Richard the Lionheart were buried there.

Mary, however, did not join this convent. Shortly after she was born, Edward, in a surviving letter, explained that his mother had the right to 'dispose of' Mary. Since her husband's death Eleanor of Provence had 'taken the veil' and was Abbess of Amesbury. In 1284, at the age of five, Mary entered her Grandmother's convent. It was not necessarily a hard life. She received an income from her mother and was the only one of Edward and Eleanor's children to attain the age of 50.

Lincoln

In 1280 the new choir at Lincoln Cathedral, built to re-house the shrine of its bishop-saint, Hugh of Avalon, was nearing completion. The shrine was translated to the Angel Choir, as it became known, by the new Bishop of Lincoln, Oliver Sutton, at the beginning of October, in the presence of Edward and Eleanor. It is claimed they were accompanied by their children, five surviving at this time, Eleanor, Joan of Acre, Alfonso, Margaret and Mary.

The Second Welsh War

In March 1282 David of Wales launched a surprise attack on England, taking Hawarden Castle, situated between Chester and Flint, capturing Roger Clifford and defeating Gilbert Clare. Edward, realising he could not afford to wait for the Feudal Host, raised mercenaries to deal with the emergency.

Llewelyn joined his brother but, on December 11th. was defeated and killed in battle. David fought on into the following year. His followers surrendered in June, and handed him over to Edward. On October 2nd. he was put to death and the brothers' heads were displayed, side by side at the Tower of London. By October 15th. in a letter to Pope Martin IV Edward was already referring to 'the late Welsh rebellion.'

Eleanor in Wales and the Marches

Eleanor accompanied her husband to Wales, giving birth to Elizabeth, their fifth daughter to survive, at Rhuddlan Castle in August 1282. Bishop Giffard of Worcester, who reported the event in a letter to the Bishop of Hereford wrote also of Edward's being at Rhuddlan with his third of the Feudal Host.

After the conflict she stayed with Edward in the Marches, sorting out problems until the middle of December. These included a poverty plea by Bishop Giffard. He claimed his diocese had been burdened by heavy expenditure by the 'coming and going of rich and poor' due to the War. The following year Eleanor was to pursue his case further in a letter to the Bishop of Tusculum, Italy. (Register of Bishop Giffard).

Acton Burnell

The Autumn Parliament or Council was held at Acton Burnell, Shropshire the main seat of Robert Burnell. Robert was well-known to both Edward and Eleanor. As a clerk of the household he had accompanied them to Gascony in 1260. Rising steadily in their service, he became Chancellor, Bishop of Bath and Wells (1275) and Archbishop Elect of Canterbury, though this office the Pope refused to confer.

Gradually, he acquired eighty-two major properties, his birth-place, Acton Burnell, being one of the first (1266). There he re-built the manor house, including a great hall, probably similar to the one he added to the Bishop's Palace at Wells. Ruins of this house with the church he built, dedicated to St. Mary, remain. The structure of this church, apart from a tower added in the 19th. century, remains much as it would have been at the time of Edward and Eleanor's visit. The ruins, administered by English Heritage, are probably those of the fortified manor house Robert obtained a licence to build in 1284. It has been suggested two end walls near the ruins are the remains of the earlier hall. (*see fig.4*). (Information from 'Acton Burnell and its Church' Salmon).

4. Acton Burnell Castle Ruins

Eleanor Acquires Property in Wales

In 1283 Edward added to his wife's ever increasing estates by granting her properties confiscated from the Welsh 'rebels'. She received, not only several Welsh manors, but David's lands and castle in Hope, near Welshpool, Powys. (Chancery Roll).

The Principality

Peaceful co-existence with Wales under vassal princes had not been achieved. In 1284 Edward sought a different solution. Wales was to become a principality.

After a tour of the North of England in January and February, Eleanor spent 1284 in Wales or on the borders. On March 18th. Edward's Statute for Wales was drawn up at Rhuddlan Castle. Canarfon was to remain the administrative centre. Here, the previous year, work had commenced on the restructuring of the Norman motte-and-bailey castle. A statue of Edward, erected over the gate of the new building was accounted the only contemporary likeness of the King to survive. It was recorded in a composite drawing by the 18th. century historian, G. Vertue.

The Court was at Canarfon from April 1st. to mid-June 1284 and it was here, on April 25th. that Eleanor's thirteenth and last child, a son Edward - to become the unfortunate King Edward II - was born. The story of how King Edward I, having promised the Welsh a prince to rule them who was born on Welsh soil and could not speak a word of English, presented them with his baby son at Canarfon, is probably untrue. It is, however, likely Edward envisaged this son as Prince of Wales, as at the time the ten year old Alfonso was heir to the English throne. Later in the year, Alfonso died and his heart was buried at the monastery of the Black Friars, London (Stow London). This did not interrupt the tour of Wales on which Edward and Eleanor had embarked. The Christmas feast and parliament were held at Bristol. This was probably the first time a king of England had celebrated a principal feast there.

Eleanor at Westminster

During May and June 1285 the Court was at Westminster. A Norwich chronicler gives a glimpse of Eleanor on May 4th. walking, in solemn procession from the Tower of London to Westminster (Abbey Church), a distance of just over 3 miles. She was accompanied by Edward, all the magnates of the realm, and 14 bishops. The Archbishop of Canterbury carried a cross, captured in Wales.

The remainder of the year was spent mainly in the South of England. That Winter Eleanor suffered the first of her winter illnesses. Medicines were paid for in December and February. In March a candle her own height was burnt as an offering for her recovery.

1286-1289

From May 1286 until August 1289 Edward and Eleanor lived abroad, in France, in Gascony and Aquitaine, visiting relations and sorting out their problems and administering their own French properties. Edward paid homage to the new King of France, Philip IV, and, in the same year, 1287, again 'took the cross'. In December Eleanor was ill with what was recorded as a 'double quartan fever'.

April, May and June 1289 were spent in Aquitaine, which Edward had inherited from his father, but, in July they visited the Viscountess of Chatellerault - probably Eleanor's cousin. The reunion must have been a pleasant one for Eleanor's accounts show she sent the Viscountess a present of scarlet cloth and ermine furs. Business was probably mixed with pleasure, as, shortly after this visit, Geoffrey de Harcourt, son of the Viscountess, was allowed his father's English estates. (J.C. Parsons 'Eleanor of Castile and the Viscountess Jeanne of Chatellerault').

Edward and Eleanor's main and most difficult diplomatic task in Europe had been to negotiate the release of the son of Charles of Anjou a prisoner of Alfonso III, King of Aragon. This had involved precarious exchanges of hostages. When all was successfully concluded, the English Court, according to a letter written by William de Hotham, Dominican Provincial and Edward's diplomatic messenger, most thankfully returned home.

Edmund, Edward's younger brother had 'supplied the King's place in England' until (a memo in the Close Rolls notes) 'August 12th. when the King arrived at Dover from Gascony and France and R. (Robert Burnell) his Chancellor arrived on the Monday preceeding from the said parts with the King's great seal'. The 'children' who had not accompanied their parents abroad were at Dover to meet Edward and Eleanor.

There was little respite. On August 14th. the Court was at Canterbury then to Leeds Castle, Rayleigh, Bury St. Edmunds, Peterborough, Westminster, Windsor, Reading, Amesbury, Clarendon etc. Christmas was celebrated at Westminster where the Court remained until the following February.

The Final Year

In March 1290 Edward and Eleanor set off over the Cotswolds to Worcestershire where they visited Feckenham, a forested estate which had been added to Eleanor's dower. They returned by way of Woodstock to Amesbury.

Family Conference (April 10th. to 17th.)

At this time there were several family matters to discuss with Edward's mother, the Prioress of Amesbury. The marriages of two of Edward and Eleanor's daughters, Joan of Acre and Margaret, were imminent. Joan, who was in her eighteenth year, had, in 1276 been betrothed to Hautman, the son of Rudolph of Hapsburg, but her fiancé had been drowned. Now, on April 30th. she was to marry Gilbert Clare, the Earl of Gloucester who had once supported Earl Simon against her father and grandfather. Margaret's marriage to John, heir of Brabant had been arranged in 1278 and was to take place on July 8th. Negotiations were in progress for the marriage between Edward of Canarfon, now approaching his seventh birthday and Margaret, the seven year old Queen of Scotland.

Arrangements had to be made for the proposed crusade - the government of the Country during Edward and Eleanor's absence and provision for the succession, should Edward fail to return.

Northern Tour

After spending May, June and most of July based at Westminster, where the two weddings were celebrated, the Court proceeded to Northampton Castle. Here the details of the Scottish marriage agreement were argued and finalised. The document was prepared for its presentation to the Michaelmas Parliament. After three tours, which included visits to Northampton Castle, Geddington Palace and Newstead Abbey, later to be associated with the poet, Byron, the Court returned to Clipstone where, in the hunting lodge, the parliament was to be held. (*see fig. 5*).

Clipstone

The hunting lodge then lay in the middle of the Crown Forest of Sherwood, which stretched from Nottingham to Worksop, covering approximately 150 square miles. In his 'Itinerary' of c.1536-1542 Leland mentions the 'woody Forest of Sherwood, where is great game of deer'. (vol.6.72.)

At Domesday the King owned 5 hides of land in Clipstone. Traditionally, King John had held court there, under an Oak tree. The jagged remains of 'Parliament Oak' may still be seen about 2 miles out of the present village on the

17

road from Ollerton to Mansfield (A6075). It stands in a grassy bay - unfortunately at the entrance to the local tip.

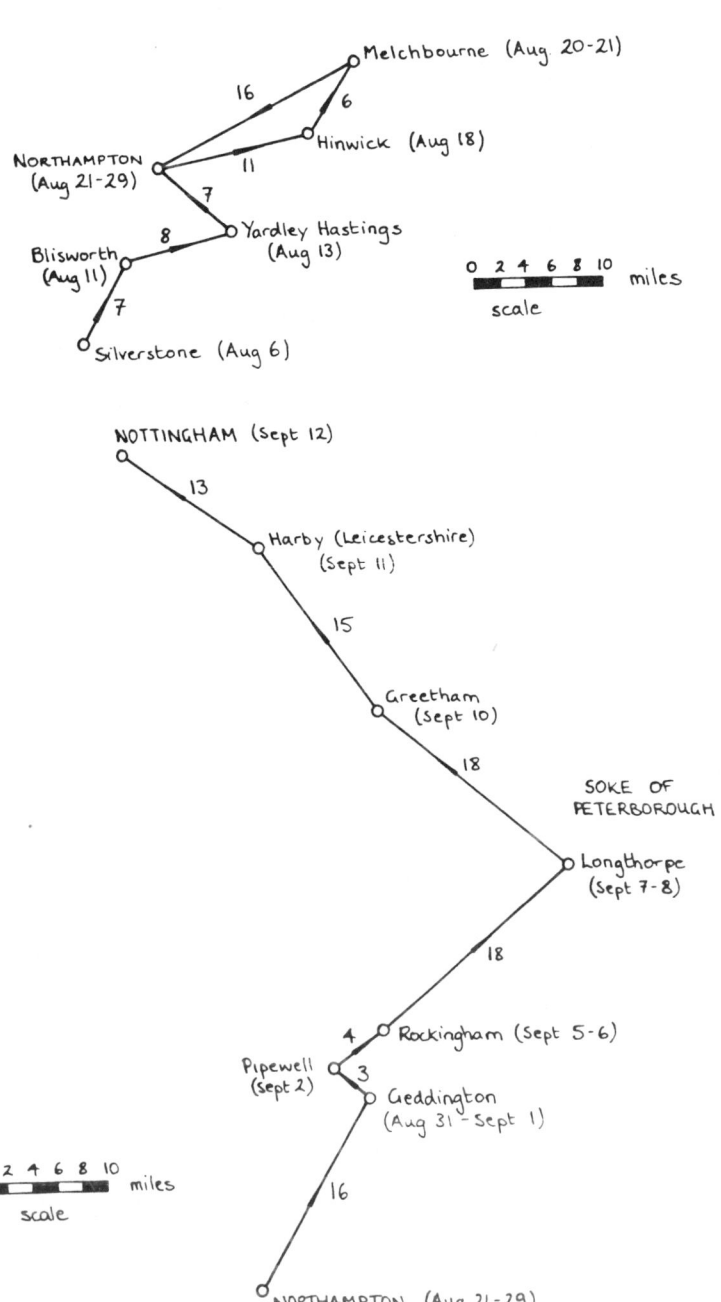

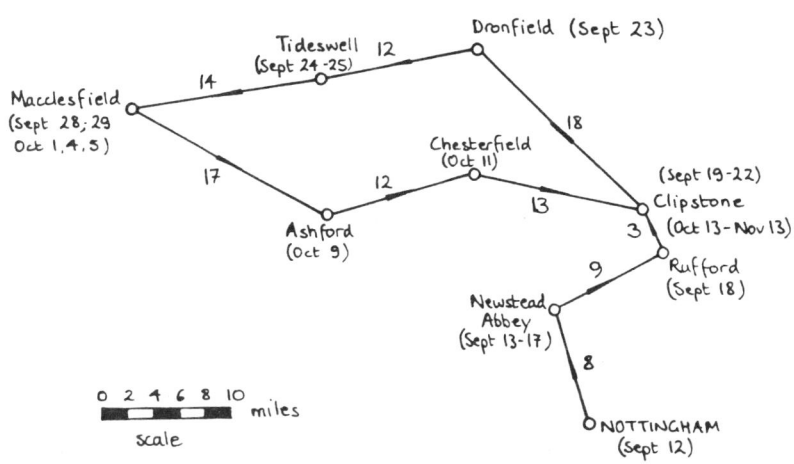

5. The Northern Tour

Evidence from Clarendon, Eleanor's manor near Salisbury and Kinver (Staffs.) suggests royal hunting lodges were considerable establishments. That at Kinver was fortified and consisted of a great hall, offices, kitchens, a royal chamber, jail and fish ponds. Orders for repairs at Clipstone (1262-1271) cover the King's mills and ponds as well as buildings. The appointment of a chaplain in 1262 suggests there was then a chapel. Regular wine deliveries imply cellar storage. Edward signed papers in his chamber. The remains of the Lodge which may still be seen in the field above 'The Dog and Duck' are of substantial walls punctuated by what appears to be a fire-place and doorways. (*see fig. 6*)

6. The Ruins of the Royal Hunting Lodge, Clipstone

The Michaelmas Parliament

The parliament at Clipstone was concerned with two major issues, the crusade and the Scottish marriage. For some time Christendom had acknowledged the necessity for a successful crusade, if the last Latin footholds in Syria were to be retained and Jerusalem and the Holy Places recaptured. A large sum, it has been estimated £130,000, had been amassed as payment to any prince undertaking the venture - a challenge Edward had accepted when he 'took the cross' in France in 1287.

The Pope who had sanctioned the agreement, died and when negotiations were opened with his successor, Nicholas IV, Edward's terms were revised to include a dispensation for the Scottish marriage.

Neither the Scottish Marriage - although the agreement was signed and sealed at Clipstone - nor the Crusade was realised. The little 'Maid of Norway' as Queen Margaret was called, died or disappeared under questionable circumstances, in the Orkney Islands, probably before the marriage contract was finalised. About 1300 a woman from Leipzig claimed to be Queen Margaret. She was burnt as a witch at Bergen. Hostilities broke out between England and Scotland, Acre fell and Edward did not lead the crusade. He and the next Pope, Boniface VIII shared the Crusade Fund between them.

The Queen's Health

Before February 1290, when William de Farendon was paid for images 'made during the Queen's illness' Eleanor had suffered her third and possibly her fourth, winter illness since 1285/6. During 1290 there were clear signs that her health was deteriorating. As well as the images - possibly ordered for her tomb - she paid £100 to the Black Friars of London for the preparation of a chapel to receive her heart. In April, a special silver vessel was bought in which to keep the Queen's syrups, suggesting these were now in constant use, and, in July, 'medicinal waters' were sent from her son Edward's household.

Although, after February there are no further hunting expenses (J.C. Parsons) Eleanor's accounts show she accompanied the King throughout the year, being on both the northern tours and at the Clipstone Parliament. The summoning of her physician, Peter of Portugal, on September 23rd. and the purchase of 'syrups and other medicines for her use' from Lincoln on October 28th. demonstrate she was far from well. When the King was at Kingston, Rufford and Laxton (Nov. 4th. - 12th.) Eleanor remained at Clipston, where he rejoined her on Nov. 12th. or 13th.

Clipstone to Harby

The last writ signed at Clipstone was dated November 13th. The Court left on November 13th. or 14th. - the date of the next writ. It was apparently heading for Lincoln. The next four places where writs were signed, Rufford, (November 14th.) Laxton (November 16th. and 17th.) Marnham (November 17th.) and Harby (November 20th. 22nd. 25th. 27th. and 28th.) all lay on a direct line between Clipstone and that town.

It took 3/4 days and a three stage journey to cover some 14 miles to Marnham and the River Trent, a pattern and speed of travel at variance with those of the usual Court itineraries. It seems likely progress was hampered by the Queen's continuing ill-health, and although it would have been preferable to have reached Lincoln, where comfortable accommodation and medical attention were available, her worsening condition enforced the stop at the Nottinghamshire village of Harby. Shelter was sought at the manor house there belonging to Richard de Weston.

Richard de Weston

By 1286 Richard de Weston was 'one of the justices appointed to deliver (suspected criminals) to the gaol of Nottingham'. Later in his career he was 'convicted before the King at Nottingham' for 'making a false record' of a delivery. On June 4th. 1293 he was pardoned 'for the salvation of the soul of Eleanor, the late Queen Consort, who died in his house at Hertheby' (Patent Rolls).

Apart from his manor at Harby, Richard held a capital messuage (manor house) and an estate of 38 acres in Marnham. In 1288 this had been sub-let for 1/8th. of a knight's fee (the cost of fielding an armed man in the King's service) and one pound of pepper (Inquisitions Post Mortem). In one of his commissions Richard is referred to as 'of Ludham' (East Anglia) so he may have held property there.

He and Agnes, his wife had also held the manor of Eagle (Eycle) near Harby, which they gave, with a wood, 80 acres of land and, at some point, a further 100 marks from Agnes, to the Templars. When Richard died, before March 1312, John, his son and heir, agreed to allow the Templars to keep these gifts in return for a yearly pension of 5 marks and annual provision for his mother out of the Eagle estate. (Close Rolls).

The Queen's Illness and Death

On November 23rd. parchment was bought in Lincoln for the wardrobe accounts and letters Eleanor intended to write. However, the purchase of 4 'urinalli' for the Queen's necessity the following day, suggests Eleanor, described as 'at that time having become infirm' had suddenly deteriorated and was confined to bed. On November 25th. a letter to Robert Tibertot of Doncaster was indeed despatched from the Queen but under the seal of Guy Ferr, who was probably acting as her household steward. (*see J.C. Parsons page 154*).

The Date of the Queen's Death

In a letter written from Ashridge to the Abbot of Cluny (France) on January 3rd. 1291, requesting prayers for the Queen's soul, Edward gave the day of Eleanor's death as 'quarto Kalend. Decembris' or November 28th. (Foedera). Westminster Abbey observed her anniversary (death) on the Eve of St. Andrew's Day. Confusion has arisen over the precise date of the death partly because the Chroniclers of Westminster and Dunstable gave the 5th day before the Kalends of December (November 27th.) and partly because the Eve of St. Andrew's day came to be regarded as the evening of November 29th. J. Hunter ('On the Death of Eleanor of Castile' in 'Archaeologia' 1842) has shown how, because the monastic day commenced at 6 p.m. the previous evening, and the eve of a saint's day was accounted the whole day, St. Andrew's Eve would have run from 6 p.m. November 28th. to 6 p.m. November 29th. and the Abbey was celebrating Eleanor's death between these hours.

The combination of Edward's secular reckoning and the Abbey's religious one places the Queen's death between 6 p.m. and mid-night on November 28th. This is verified by the Queen's household accounts for 1290, wherein the words 'Decessus Regine' are entered at the end of the transactions for November 28th.

Post Mortem (in consultation with Dr. Christine Solomon)

A likely cause of Eleanor's death was phthisis. A modern equivalent of this is T.B. of the lung. The Queen's symptoms appear as a fever - the 'double quartan' of the letter written from France in December 1287 and the 'low fever' which the writer of the Osney Chronicle claims caused her death (J.C. Parsons) - together with a persistant cough, suggested by the regular supply of 'syrups'.

The progress of the illness in relation to time, location and climate is also compatible with a diagnosis of T.B. Temporary relief in the Winter of 1288/9 could have resulted from the Queen's sojourn in France, particularly in the Pyrenees. Early this century, before effective medication, mountain air was found to benefit sufferers from lung T.B.

The deterioration during the Autumn of 1290 could have been the result of Eleanor's 'Northern Tour', the strain of which, together with a potentially cold and damp terrain and climate, may have aggravated her condition. The brief 'recovery' at Harby on November 23rd. when the Queen felt capable of writing letters and sent to Lincoln for parchment, and her sudden relapse and death, are not uncommon in the terminal stages of this illness.

Two surviving images of Eleanor, that on the outside of Lincoln Cathedral (see cover) and Torel's tomb statue at Westminster, demonstrate a physical change. The former is of a matronly figure with full 'typically Spanish' face, whereas, in the latter, the features are thin and the figure reduced. If these images were representative of the Queen's appearance at the relevant times, they would offer evidence of a physical change, also in keeping with the ravages of pthisis.

The Eleanor Chantry at Harby

No church is recorded in Domesday Harby, but the village possessed one in September 1290 when Edward, at Nottingham, ordered 'Master William de Kelm, parson of the church at Herdeby to have from the Forest of Sherwood, 4 good oak trees fit for timber with their strippings of the King's gift.' (Close).

After Eleanor's death, Edward established a chantry in the Church at Harby. Ten marks were to be paid annually to the chantry priest to pray for her soul. The manor of Navenby, 8 miles south of Lincoln, was given for the chantry's maintenance. This manor, held by the Abbot and Convent of Fecamp (Normandy) was released to Lincoln Cathedral, responsible for the administration of this chantry, on April 28th. 1292. Eleanor's chantry was abolished during the reign of Edward VI.

Harby Today

An earlier church, restored in 1820 was demolished. Cornelius Brown quotes Thosby (Thoroton) describing a small single-aisled building of stone with massive walls. This may have been the 1290 church. The present church was built in 1876.

A brass plate in the floor of the chancel is inscribed 'Here died Eleanor of Castile, Queen of England. November 27th. A.D. 1290'. Outside, on the church tower, under the clock, a statue of Eleanor is flanked by four coats of arms. It was copied from her tomb effigy in Westminster Abbey and given by Mr. Freeth, a 19th. century antiquarian. (*see fig. 7*). Outside the churchyard details of Eleanor's life and a pictorial representation of her funeral cortege are shown on a notice board.

7. Harby Church

Richard Weston's House

The manor house in which Eleanor spent her last days no longer stands. Its overgrown foundations and the indentations of a ditch or moat may be seen in a field behind the Church. (*see fig. 8*).

8. The Site of Richard Weston's House

PART II

The Journey to Westminster

Travel in 1290

The Queen's body had to be transported from Harby to Westminster Abbey. Her cortège would have had to contend with those general problems which beset the late 13th. century traveller.

Much of the countryside in 1290 was forested and the forests were inhabited not only by a limited number of outlaws and robbers (most manors kept the peasant work-force on a tight rein) but by wolves. In 1296, John Engaine was granted the manor of Laxton in return for defending four counties, including Northamptonshire and Nottinghamshire, against wolves.

There was no drainage programme and large areas of the countryside, particularly about Lincoln, were marshy or subject to flooding. Roads which avoided flood plains usually offered a circuitous route and lengthened journey. An answer to the problems of marsh and flood had been to raise roads on causeways. Many of the Roman and/or pre-roman roads still in use had been raised, where necessary, in this way.

Medieval roads were subjected to heavy traffic and had to be maintained. This responsibility fell variously upon the religious houses, the local manors or the King. It was a burden few accepted willingly. A writ issued to the Prior of Dunstable in 1285 illustrates the problem. Edward had 'learnt' that the high roads (Watling Street and Ickneild Street - A5 and A505) passing through Dunstable were 'so broken up and rutted by the constant passage of carts that dangerous injuries threaten those passing by those roads.' (Annales of the Prior of Dunstable). The King, wishing to avoid such injuries himself, ordered instant repairs, pointing out it was the responsibility of the Prior and vill by custom, and threatening to apply 'a heavier hand than this' if the repairs were not speedily executed.

The condition or absence of bridges created further problems for the 13th. century traveller. Bridge building and maintenance were skilled and expensive processes and bridges, once fallen, could remain so, forcing travellers to resort to the old ford or a ferry service.

The European order of Bridge Friars, responsible for the bridge at Avignon, amongst others, did not become established in England.

Other religious houses might build and maintain bridges for their own use, such as that at Stamford, which connected the properties of St. Peter's, Burgh, lying on both sides of the River Welland, but, faced with the expenses of providing constant and almost limitless hospitality, most religious houses must have considered the maintenance of a bridge not for monastic use low priority. Solutions were to grant indulgences for the work, to impose it as a penance, or to pay a small pension to a bridge warden who would keep the bridge in order and possibly ask charity or demand tolls from its users to supplement the pension.

Certain bridges relied on tollage alone. Ominously, control of this was seen as a desirable asset. William Latimer of Yarm begged the tollage of the bridge of Yarm (across the River Tees) from Edward, adding to his petition

'May it please him to do this for the soul of Madame his consort' (Eleanor).

The King's reply was favourable. The lucrative tolls on London Bridge had been granted to Edward's mother, who had taken the money and ignored the responsibilities. The bridge was severely damaged, as were many others, by the frost and snow of 1280/1. (Stow Annales). Edward launched a disaster fund - a levy throughout the Kingdom - 'on account of the catastrophe which has happened'. (Patent Rolls). Aid came too late. Five arches of the Bridge fell.

Transport by Water

Rivers were widely used for internal transport in 13th. century England. Inevitably, certain waters, meandering, silting up, impeded by low, narrow-arched bridges, without a hinged span, were unsuitable for larger craft. Others, those of the Thames, Avon, Severn, Humber and Trent were extensively used for cargoes, particularly those difficult to transport by road such as wine and lead.

The waterway serving Lincoln encompassed the Rivers Humber and Trent, the Foss Dyke or Roman Canal and part of the River Witham, which divided Southern Lincoln from the suburb of Wigford.

The Roman Canal

The Roman Canal (Foss Dyke) had been constructed, probably during the Roman occupation of Britain to join the River Trent to the River Witham at Lincoln. The Witham entered from the East. The waters of the Canal and River mingled in a wide stretch of water known as Bradeford - now used as a Marina.

Viability of the System during the 13th. Century

Simeon, the annalist of Durham, recorded that the Canal was reopened for traffic in 1121. It had silted up again before Bishop Atwater of Lincoln's (1514-1521) cleaning programme (Leland) but Defoe in his 'Tour through the Whole Island of Great Britain' Vol.2 (1735-1742) found the Canal 'useful to the trade of the City'. The state of the Canal apparently responded to the commercial prosperity of the Town, so it was likely to have been in use during the active trading of the 13th. century.

From Bradeford the River Witham turned South, running through the suburb of Wigford near to St. Katherine's Priory. This part of the system appears to have been operative in the fourteenth century. A complaint made by the Prior in 1333 refers to the removal of four ships from the Priory quay at 'Timberland' (Patent).

Court Travel

In spite of improvements in domestic comfort introduced by Edward's father at certain royal castles and hunting lodges and by some abbots and bishops in their own residences during the 13th. century, even for the Court furniture and utensils were in short supply. Local manor houses were even less well equipped.

On itineraries, a degree of comfort was assured by the baggage train, which accompanied the Court, carrying furnishing, clothes, equipment and provisions. The Household Ordinance stipulated the number of carts assigned to the various household departments and sub-departments. In 1286 the royal baggage train had consisted of 6 long carts, 6 short carts and pack animals to carry valuables and things required for immediate use (such as the King's breakfast).

The Court was organised to be constantly on the road. Even so, Edward and Eleanor's arrival at Harby and at least one week stay must have created problems for both the court officials and the local population. The laden carts of the baggage train would not have taken kindly to the country lanes. They were probably stood off or sent on by main roads to Lincoln, essentials being transported to the Manor House by pack horse or peasant power. It is unlikely the Manor House possessed more than one bed- the Lord and Lady's. However, Richard de Weston may not have been at Harby during the Court stay, otherwise Edward might have recognised him at Nottingham. If not, at least the Lord's private apartment, were there one, could have been used without causing too much inconvenience. The King's sergeants no doubt exacted supplies from Harby and the nearby manors or they were fetched from the Lincoln markets.

Organising the Cortège

From Harby the Court sergeants faced an additional transport problem. The Queen's body had to be carried with decorum, safety and reasonable speed. A suitable carriage had to be provided. Later, at Dunstable, a 'feretrum' - a litter or bier which could be borne by men or beasts - was mentioned.

This journey had to be organised to fulfil different needs from the regular itinerary. Suitable overnight accommodation for the Court must now include a church where the body of the Queen might lie before the altar and a vigil kept with appropriate prayers and services. The body was to be embalmed and three funerals held, for which the completed preparations must synchronise with the arrival of the cortège. It is possible the route was planned to incorporate certain places associated with the Queen. The first three towns, Lincoln, Grantham and Stamford had all been part of her dower, Lincoln having been added in 1275 (Charter Roll). They were also on the main road to London.

Winter and Darkness

The cortège left Harby at the end of November or beginning of December. With lighting limited to fires and torches, broken roads and the dire example of Edward's brother-in-law, Alexander of Scotland, who, five years before, journeying in darkness against all advice, had been killed when his horse stumbled, travel by night was to be avoided. The hours of daylight were limited, reducing, and dependant on the weather.

Then, as now, the weather in England appears to have been variable. Annalists recorded unusually severe climatic conditions. As nothing emerges for Winter 1290 it was probably a moderate one. However, the relative speed at which the cortège completed the first part of the journey (see Digest of the Cortège Route) suggests bad weather or some other impediment was feared.

The Cortège Route

There has been some disagreement over the main route followed by the Queen's cortege from Harby to Westminster Abbey Church, where her final burial took place. The backbone of the journey can be established from the King's writs and letters and the sites of the Queen's memorial (Eleanor) crosses. (*see fig. 1*).

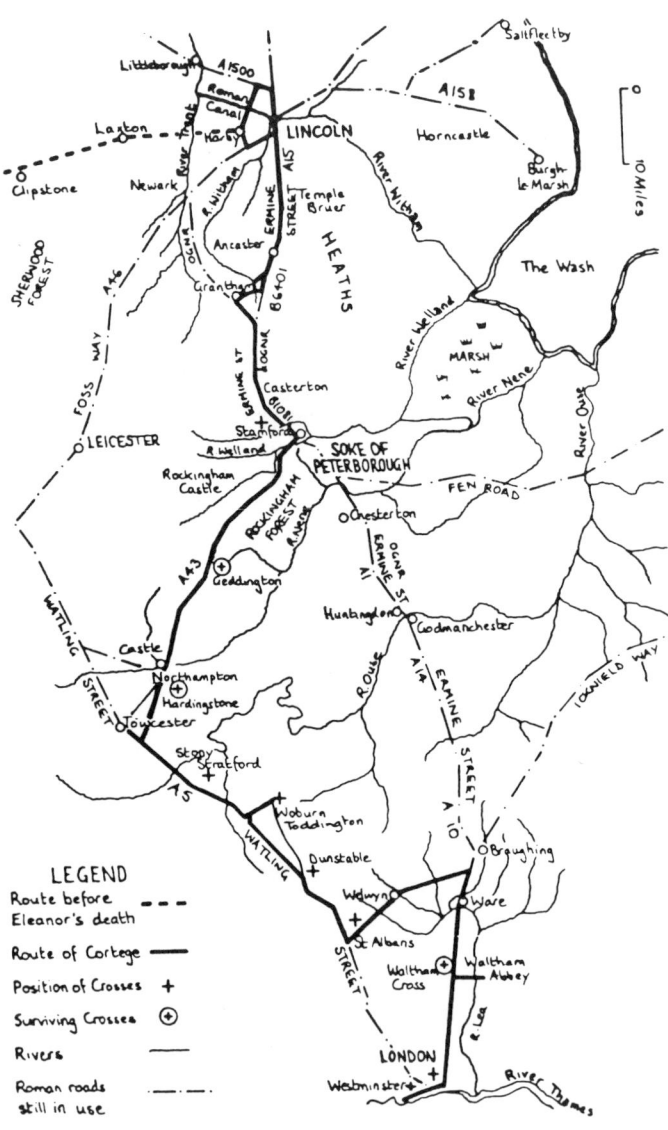

1. The Journey to Westminster
Route map drawn by Dr. W. Powrie.

The 'Eleanor Crosses'

According to the Chronicler of St. Alban's 'in every place or vill in which the body rested the Lord King commanded a wonderful cross to be set up.'

The Chronicler of Dunstable Priory describes the method of site selection:-

'When the body of the said Queen (Eleanor) was departing from Dunstable, the bier was set down in the centre of the Market Place while the King's Chancellor (Robert Burnell) and the great men there and those present had marked a suitable place where they might afterwards erect, at royal expense, a cross of wonderful size, our Prior (William de Wederow) being present and sprinkling Holy Water'.

The combined evidence of these two extracts suggests the Crosses indicated the settlement where the Cortège stopped, but not the precise building where the night was spent. Considering the size of the Court, it was unlikely that a single place was always sufficient to accommodate all the departments. As it emerges later, a 'suitable place' for the cross meant the most public, where the cross could be seen by the maximum number of people, markets, major roads and junctions. There is evidence for twelve crosses. Nine are recorded in the Accounts of Queen Eleanor's Executors. That at Geddington, though not referred to by name in the accounts, having survived, is very much a reality. Grantham and Stamford crosses are mentioned in local records. More detailed evidence for the lost crosses will be given later in the text.

During the journey the King signed writs or letters at Harby (November 28th.) Lincoln (December 2nd. and 3rd) Great Casterton (near Stamford December 5th.) Northampton (December 9th.) St. Alban's (December 13th.) London (December 14th. and 15th.) Westminster (burial December 17th.)

The route is now given with alternative ways, present road numbers, 1290 town layouts and remains for those wishing, in reality or in the imagination, to follow the way of the Queen's Cortège.

Three Ways to Lincoln (*see fig. 2*)

Harby lay (and lies) barely six miles due west of Lincoln's southern suburb, Wigford. There was no direct route from Harby to the medieval city. Lincoln had been built on a limestone ridge, rising some 200 feet above the River Witham, making for a difficult access from the western plain on which Harby was situated. The wooded nature of the terrain in 1290 would have made it advisable for the Cortège to adhere to the established ways.

The Roman road, Ermine Street, also one of the major medieval roads, ran through Lincoln from North to South. From the South-west the Foss Way (A46) crossed the Witham, joining Ermine Street just South of Lincoln, probably at Bracebridge which had been a Domesday manor. Margery (Roman Roads in Britain) gives another Roman road entering from the North-west (Bawtry), crossing the Trent at Littleborough (Segelocum) and joining Ermine Street North of Lincoln. Part of this road has survived in the A1500. Another 13th. century way into Lincoln was by the Roman Canal, which ran North of Harby. A network of minor roads gave Harby and its surrounding medieval settlements access to each other and these main ways to Lincoln.

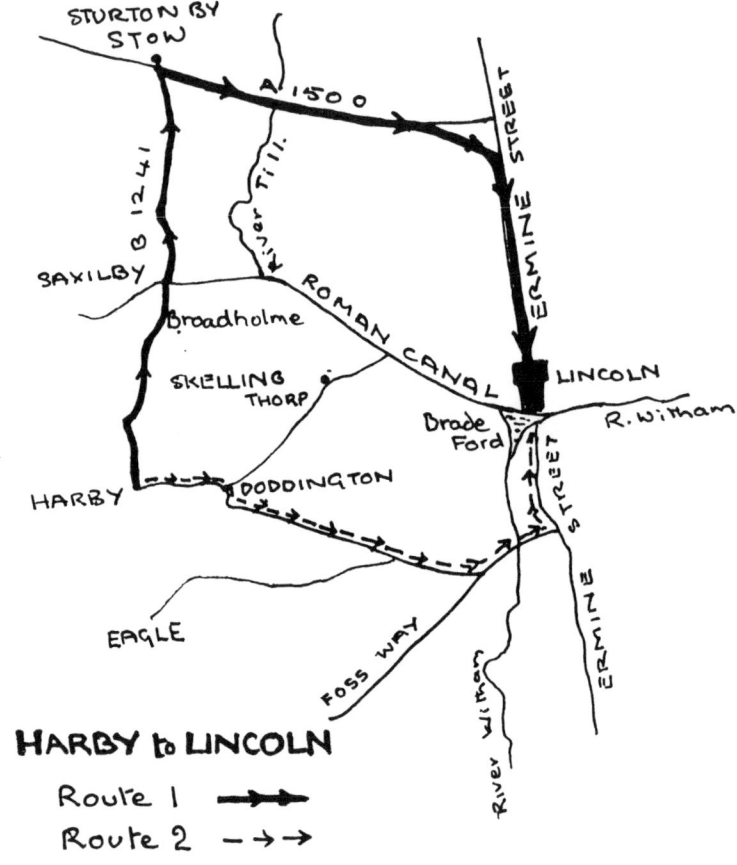

2. 3 Ways to Lincoln

West, North or South?

In 1290 Lincoln was a walled town with a gate access. From Harby entry through its North and West gates could only be gained by crossing the Roman Canal.

The Canal Crossing

It is not certain where viable crossings of the Canal lay in this section at the time, but a bridge connecting the Priory of Broadholme with the Domesday manor of Saxilby, where the A56 crosses today, is most likely. There may also have been a ferry service for foot travellers between the Domesday manors of Skellingthorpe and Burton. This could only have been serviced by a small boat and, consequently was unsuitable for the transport needs of the Cortège.

Western Access

Assuming the Cortège crossed the Canal, it is unlikely it would have entered Lincoln by the western gates. The West town gate to the northern sector of the city was probably re-blocked by 1290 (see The Fair of Lincoln) leaving the only access on that side a small postern in the castle wall. The more southerly of the western gates gave an entry to the town less than 300 yards from the South gate, which was far more easily accessible from Harby.

Northern Access

Eventually the Court needed to reach the northern part of the Town, the administrative centre which offered the most sophisticated and secure accommodation and where the Cathedral was situated. If the Cortège crossed the Canal it could only have been to arrive in Lincoln through the North gate.

From Harby the route to the Canal passed the Priory of Broadholme, situated on the site of Manor Farm. It was a small convent of Premonstratensian nuns. This order, founded at Premontre (France) by St. Norbert, was shaped into a contemplative order by the Saint's successor, Hugh de Fosses. Its devotees dressed in bleached wool, which gave them the name of White Canons, and followed a strict daily routine of sung offices, fasting, silence and manual labour. A Lincolnshire baron, Peter de Goxhill had introduced them into England in 1143. (Medieval Monasticism C.H. Lawrence).

After crossing the Canal the route ran through Saxilby and Ingleby to Sturton by Stow, all three Domesday manors (B1241). Here, it turned East along the Roman Road, crossing the River Till, to Ermine Street. (This Roman Road equates with the A15 but diverges just before the junction with the B1398). Ermine Street (A15) entered Lincoln by the Roman North Gate or Newport Arch. (*see fig. 2*).

The main disadvantages of this route were the distance from Harby to Lincoln Cathedral 24.5km. as opposed to the 14.5km. of the southern route and the likelihood of 3.5km. of poor road from Harby to Broadholme Priory. The latter would have been off-set by the possibility of a reasonable road from the Priory to Sturton (6.5km.) and good roads from Sturton to the Cathedral (14.5km.)

The route had an advantageous social aspect. The Priory and manors could have given sustenance, spread the news of the Queen's death and offered prayers for her soul. The North gate would have provided an impressive framework for a ceremonial arrival, but the real advantage of this Northern route was that it gave immediate access to the Northern sector of the Town by manageable gradients.

Southern Access

The southern route into Lincoln ran from Harby eastwards to its neighbouring manor of Doddington.

Doddington and Skellingthorpe

At Domesday, Doddington was described as 'a manor of St. Peter's Westminster' (Westminster Abbey). Skellingthorpe was disputed - Baldwin claiming it from the King, and the Abbot as part of the Doddington estate.

In 1281 John Picot and his heirs had been granted free warren (right to hunt specific animals) of all his desmesne lands in Doddington. His neighbour, Walter de Stirchesle and Alice his wife were granted free warren of their lands in 'Skeldingthorp' in 1283, keeping up with the Picots.

From Doddington a road of Roman straightness - probably a 'monks' way' - ran to the Roman Foss (A46). Crossing the River Witham, the Foss joined Ermine Street, not here truly represented by the modern road system, and ran through the suburb of Wigford to Lincoln's more southern gate.

The road from Harby to Doddington is likely to have been poor, but from Doddington to the Town gate the roads should have been good. The serious disadvantage of this route was the gradient of Steep Hill dividing the northern sector from the South of the Town. This would have been difficult on foot, undesirable for the Cortège, and virtually - though perhaps not quite (*see fig. 3*) - impossible for transport.

A southern entry could also have been effected by way of the Canal itself. This would not have effaced the problem of Steep Hill, and the journey required to reach the Canal with the loading and unloading required do not make this an attractive solution.

3. A Reaper's cart going up hill

NEWPORT IN 1290

The Augustine Friary

If the cortège had taken the northern route to Lincoln it would have passed through the suburb of Newport which was developing along both sides of Ermine Street, outside the North Gate of the City. Leland, writing of this suburb 1534-1542 found there was then:-
'No noticeable thing but the ruins of a house of Augustine friars on the South side.'
This friary is likely to have been the 'Graye friers' shown on the edge of Speed's town map (*see fig. 4*), situated on the west side of Ermine Street. It was destroyed at the Dissolution. The site had covered c. 4 acres (V.C.H.)

The Rule of St. Augustine was accepted and adapted by several religious entities, including the military orders. Hermits were organized into an Augustine order by 1250.

The 'Austin' friars were established in Newport by 1270, when they were granted wood for building their church. This was finished by 1291 when they requested a licence for its consecration from Bishop Oliver Sutton of Lincoln.

'Newport Church'

During the 13th. century two churches are recorded in Newport, St. Nicholas and St. John the Baptist. Leland noted a church 'without the North-east corner tower of the town wall', probably the 'Newport Church' of Speed's town plan. As this church survived the Dissolution it is likely to have been the parish church, identified in 'Medieval Lincoln' (Hill) as that dedicated to St. Nicholas - the patron saint of children. It would have stood on the corner of the A15 and Church Lane and would have been passed by the Cortège provided the Northern entry was used.

A church dedicated to John the Baptist was recorded in Newport in 1229. This saint was the patron of the Templars (founded 1118) and the Knights of St. John or Hospitallers (founded c. 1092). Both these military orders held property in Lincoln and this church may have been monastic. It is not recorded by either Leland or Speed and may have not survived to 1290.

St. Giles (Egidu)

475 paces East of 'Newport Church' Speed's map shows the Hospital of St. Giles, the first of the medieval hospitals on the route. Such hospitals were primarily for the sick and poor and were usually allowed to continue - often as alms-houses - after the Dissolution, so throughout the Country, several have survived. The usual appearance and layout of these hospitals may be seen in St. Mary's Chichester founded before 1229 still in use and open to the public. A single storey church-like building housed a long hall with beds down each side, a living space in the middle and a chapel at the end. The whole was in the keeping of a Master.

The Mastership of St. Giles had been annexed to Lincoln Cathedral by Oliver Sutton during his period as Dean (i.e. before 1280). St. Giles, also known as St. Egidu, the patron saint of beggars and cripples was favoured by the Benedictine orders, so the Hospital may have had early associations with the Benedictine Cathedral. It became a refuge for needy clergy and was extended into the 'L' shaped structure shown on Speed's map. St. Giles did not survive but according to Pevsner one reconstructed 12th. century doorway and the arch to a side chapel used in the present St. Giles, Lamb Gardens, were taken from the old St. Giles Hospital.

LINCOLN IN 1290

The Roman Settlement and Southern Extension

Leland claimed Lincoln was 'built three times' and three distinct areas of the town may still be identified, the Roman settlement on the hill top, a southerly extension to the River Witham and the suburb of Wigford. (*see fig. 4*).

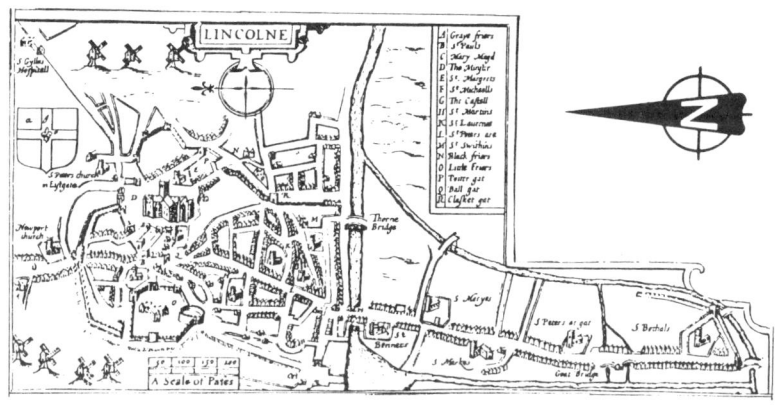

4. Speed's Map

The Roman Settlement, established c.85-96 A.D. had been enclosed by quadrilateral walls, each with a central gate. These had been rebuilt, probably in the third century, when the South wall had been breached to allow the city's southern extension. In 1217 the North, East and West walls had all still been in use.

The North gate spans the road at the end of Bailgate (here 'gate' meaning road) before it widens into the Newport Road (Ermine Street A15). Parts of the wall have also survived, in a garden, on the west side of the Gate, below ground level. (*see fig. 5*).

5. Newport Arch

Under William the Conqueror, a castle had been built in the south-west corner of the Roman wall. The Roman West Gate, then standing c. 4 yards to the north-west of this castle's outer defences, was infilled before 1217, and, with the remainder of the west wall, continued to serve as part of the city's defence system. (*see fig. 6*).

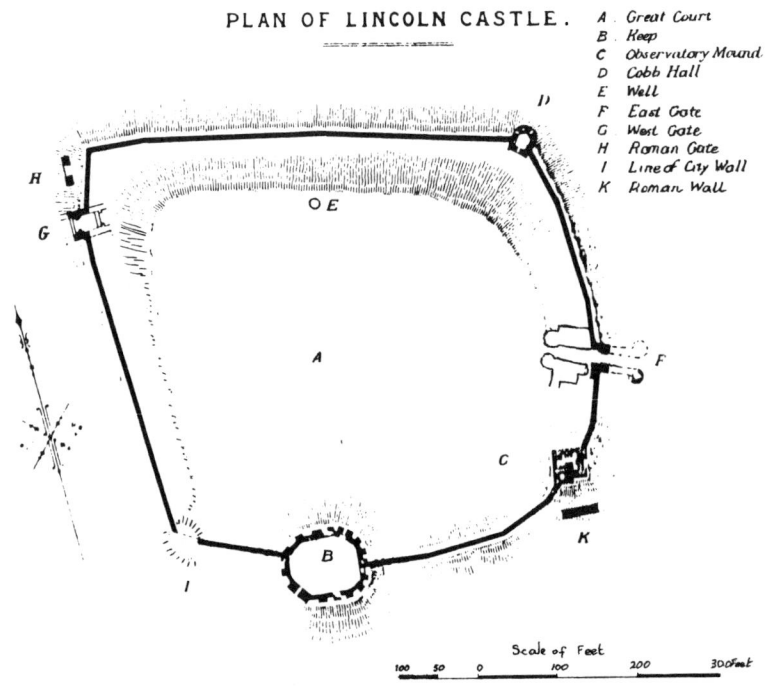

6. Plan of Lincoln Castle

The 'Fair of Lincoln'

When the Castle was being beseiged from inside the town by the supporters of King Louis of France in 1217, the in-filled west gate (H) was breached, allowing William Marshal with troops loyal to the boy-king Henry III to enter the town. Skirting the Castle wall, they gained the open space, then existing between the Castle and the Cathedral. The beseigers were engaged and defeated. This battle became known as the 'Fair of Lincoln'.

The West Gate was re-closed, and probably not in use in 1290, although an opening in the wall near this point is shown in Speed's town map of c.1610. In 1836 the gate was dug out and an attempt made to open it, but the arch collapsed and the remains of the gate were removed.

Shortly after the erection of the Norman castle the building of a Minster, almost immediately to become a Cathedral (Bishop's seat) was commenced in the south-east corner of the Roman Settlement. Between 1133 and 1148 the East Gate with land was granted to the third Norman bishop of Lincoln, Alexander of Blois, who resided in the East gate tower.

An excavation of the East Gate site from 1964 to 1966 revealed an 80 foot ditch and evidence of four successive structures - three Roman and one medieval. The site has been left open and the remains of this gate may be seen in front of East Gate Hotel.

The easterly extension of the Cathedral (1256-1280) necessitated moving the east wall south of this gate. This was authorised by a letter from King Henry III. The east wall's displacement is reflected in the shape of the Cathedral's eastern precinct.

There was an interval tower on the wall between the east and north gates. This was probably the 'great ruin of a tower in the town wall' noted by Leland on the East side of Newport Gate and suburb.

The South gate to the early Roman Settlement stood on Steep Hill - just before the ground begins to drop away. On September 30th. 1745 Stukeley wrote in his diary 'I observe they have now pulled down the huge stones of the Roman gate on the South side of the old city. The arch was destroyed by Houghton, the jailor, a good many years ago'. (Diaries and Letters Vol. 1 p.317). G.T. Clark, addressing the Lincoln Doicescan Architectural Society in June 1875 claimed one jamb of this gate then remained. This is probably the area of dressed stone (c.10 foot by three foot) incorporated into the wall to the North side of number 25 Steep Hill. A street lamp is fixed in the brick wall at this point.

The Castle and the Cathedral

In 1290 the Castle and the Cathedral, established in the Roman Settlement, were sited as they are to-day, though both have altered structurally throughout the intervening 700 years.

The Castle in 1290

At Domesday, 166 dwellings were no longer taxable as they had been destroyed to permit the building of the Norman castle. The layout of the original motte (mound) and bailey (courtyard) castle is still discernible.

7. Building a Motte from the Bayeux Tapestry

    In late 11th. century castle construction, when an artificial motte was required the usual procedure was to dig a circular ditch throwing the excavated earth into the centre to create the mound. (*see fig. 7*). A wooden tower was then raised on this mound and a wooden palisade erected on the inner circumference of the ditch. Further protection was usually provided by an outer bailey.

    The castle at Lincoln appears to have been a typical example and there is no reason to believe the positions of the motte, inner-bailey walls and main gate have been radically altered. An area referred to as the bailey in 1229 could have initially been this castle's outer bailey. If so, before that date, when John de Bondeby gave 'all his land' and 'all his houses thereon' to the Church of St. Mary Barlings, the outer bailey had passed into private hands. Leland mentions Bail Gate as a 'poor little gate, by South a little this side of the Minster'.

    During the 12th. century, wooden defensive structures, vulnerable to fire and war machines, were replaced by keeps and curtain walls of stone. Where an artificial motte was insufficiently compacted to bear the weight of heavy masonry, either the keep was raised on new, solid ground or, as at Lincoln, the wooden palisade was replaced by a high stone wall to form a 'shell' keep. Lincoln's stone palisade wall, now much reduced in height, has survived as 'Lucy Tower'. Tradition connects this structure with a Lucy who was Constable of the Castle from 1114 to 1140. Repairs were ordered by the King for a 'Tour de Luce' in 1225. (*see fig. 8*).

The main gate was also found to be a weakness of the castle defence system, and a tower was sometimes erected as additional protection. At Lincoln, the remnant of such a tower constitutes the rectangular base of the 'Observatory Tower'. The main (east) castle gate at Lincoln, (F) supplied with a portcullis and draw-bridge, was also provided with a barbican, usually a double towered gate raised before the main gate. The barbican was removed in 1791.

8. Lucy Tower at Lincoln Castle

In 1227 King Henry III had ordered the Sheriff to survey the Castle gates which he had heard were broken. As a result repairs were ordered and the 'tower of the Great Gate to be completed'. It would appear the work continued beyond 1229 when 20 marks were allotted to set up a kiln in the Castle grounds.

Towards the end of the 13th. century the weaknesses of square towers and keeps became apparent and round towers were introduced, a trend demonstrated in the 'welsh castles' of Edward I. A round tower which allowed the defenders a freer range and vision, could be added to the outer walls of older castles. The curved tower on the north-east wall at Lincoln, now known as 'Cobb Hall' survives as an example of this development but it may have been erected shortly after 1290.

Buildings of the Inner Bailey

In 1290 the castle was essentially a fortress and when necessary a prison, but there is an earlier reference to repairing houses there (1227). It is likely these domestic buildings were of wood and thatch and situated in the Inner Bailey.

There was also a chapel in the Castle before 1267 when it was to be repaired 'against the King's coming'. The following year a chaplain was engaged to celebrate (Mass) for the King's ancestors.

Castle Constables in 1290

For much of its early history the Castle had been held by Constables for the Crown, two of whom had been women. Lucy, a descendant of Leofric, Earl of Mercia and his more famous wife the Lady Godiva, had married Ivo de Taillebois, one of William's barons. In 1114, their daughter, also Lucy, claimed the hereditary constableship. During the conflict between King Stephen and the Empress Matilda, this Lucy's son by her second marriage, Ranulph Gernons, Earl of Chester, seized the Castle. Stephen attempted to regain possession. In the resulting battle, known as the 'Joust of Lincoln' (1141) Stephen was taken prisoner. On regaining his liberty, Stephen deprived Ranulph of the Castle but restored it to him in the general amnesty of 1151.

Richard de Hay held the Castle as a sub-tenant from another Earl of Chester, Ranulph de Blundeville, who was also Earl of Lincoln. Richard's daughter, Nicola a supporter of King John, was both Constable of the Castle and Sheriff of Lincolnshire. She held the castle when its seige was relieved by the 'Fair of Lincoln' in 1217.

Between 1227 and 1229 a Robert de Tatteshale was paid 60 shillings a year for his duties as Constable of the Castle. After Ranulph de Blundeville's death in 1232 the Castle and Earldom passed by marriage to the Lacy family. Henry Lacy, a staunch supporter of Edward I was Earl of Lincoln from 1272 to 1311. Recorded as Constable of the Castle in 1310, and likely to have been so in 1290, he was also one of the executors of Queen Eleanor's will.

Later History of the Castle

In 1644, during the Civil War, the Castle was taken by storm. Defoe (c.1725) describes it as a ruin. It was restored to become a prison and present buildings within the bailey were constructed during the 19th. century to accommodate prisoners and guards.

The Cathedral in 1290

The Norman Cathedral had initially consisted of a nave with transepts, a tower, raised on the crossing and a short apsidal choir. It suffered the usual traumas of earthquake and fire. Of the Norman Cathedral, the great portals and West towers up to the third storey, remain.

By 1290 the choir had undergone two extensions, which had left the tower west of centre. The second of these was the 'Angel Choir' where Edward and Eleanor had attended the ceremony conducted by Bishop Oliver Sutton. It is claimed the figures of Edward and Eleanor on the South external wall commemorated this event, and there is much in the stance and draperies of the figures to support this claim, although they must have been restored many times. (*see cover*). A 57 foot high East window inserted in 1288 has not survived.

Other 13th. century changes and additions to the main fabric were the facing to the West front, the building of a Chapter House from 1220 onwards, a 'Galilee' (porch) to the South transept c.1250, and the replacement of the collapsed tower by 1256. The 13th. century tower was low, standing only as far as the first storey of the present one. A full account of the Cathedral's architecture may be found in 'Lincolnshire' in 'The Buildings of England' series.

The Cathedral Precincts

In 1285, a request to enclose the Cathedral precincts to protect the Dean and Chapter from 'night attacks when passing from their houses to the Minster', made by Bishop Oliver Sutton, was granted. A wall, 12 foot high, was to be raised in 'suitable places at Pottergate Street, and the street leading from the High Road to the Bailey to the East Gate, with two adjoining lanes in the North side'. Sufficient gates were to be provided, which were to be locked at sunset and opened at sunrise. Part of the precinct wall, running from South of Potter Gate, crossing two lanes to East Gate, enclosing the North-east segment, may be seen on Speed's map. (*see fig. 4*).

Although the gateway known as Pottergate (*see fig. 9*) has been attributed to the 14th. century, it is likely this was one of the 'sufficient gates' of the 13th. century precinct enclosure.

In 1285 there must have been houses for the Dean and Chapter in the Cathedral precincts as the wall was designed to protect the way between them and the Cathedral, but, apart from possibly one window in the South range of Vicars' Court (founded by Bishop Oliver Sutton at the end of the 13th. century) which it is claimed in Pevsner is in a 'form possible before 1299' virtually nothing of the 1290 precinct building has survived.

9. Pottergate

The Southern Extension

Long before the building of the Norman Castle and Minster, possibly as early as the third century, the southern wall of the Roman city had been breached and the town extended towards the River Witham, Bradeford and the Roman Canal. This extension had been protected by three new walls with gates.

Walls and Gates

The new South Gate, was on the site of the present Stonebow and Guildhall (renovated 1887). About the fourth century a postern was cut into the South wall, East of Stonebow, at the River end of what is now Bank Street. Excavations have shown this gate to have been 6 foot wide and built from older cut stone. Its remains, together with a stretch of the South wall, are preserved in the basement of William and Glyn's Bank and may be seen by arrangement with the City and County Museum ("Beneath the Strongbow Centre"). It was unlikely the 'postern on the South' was in use in 1290, as it had been blocked by the Grey Friars in 1258.

The West Gate has also been excavated and the remains may be seen at City Hall, Orchard Street. The Clasket Gate of Speed's map was probably the East Gate, giving access to what is now Monks' Road.

Water seems to have been both the blessing and the scourge of the Southern Extension.
'I heard say that the lower part of Lincoln town was all marsh, and won by policy and inhabited for the commodity of the water', wrote Leland. In Defoe's time the River flowed 'sometimes into the street'. But the waterways were useful to the merchants and this was 'the best part of the City for trade and business'.

In the High Market, at the top of Steep Hill, produce and skins could be bought. On the west, in the Parish of St. Michael on the Hill, now recalled in Michael Gate, ran Parchemine Gate, which suggests here the complex processes by which skins are turned to parchment were executed. Here, no doubt, parchment for Eleanor's last letter was bought. St. Martin's Church, remembered in St. Martin's Street, lay "in the Cloth Market". The Mint, operational since the reign of Alfred had been closed down by Edward, but the allied Jewellery Quarter survived. There must have been alehouses to supply the traders, but these are impossible to trace as they were no more than private houses distinguished by the sign of a broom.

The Jewish Community

Before 1290 there appears to have been a firm Jewish presence in the Southern Extension, and, to a lesser degree, in the suburb of Wigford. In 1257 King Henry had re-allocated the tenancies of properties which had been held by Leo, son of Solomon, Jacob, son of Leo, and Vives of Northampton, Jews who had been hanged for the supposed ritual murder of a Christian boy, subsequently known as Little St. Hugh. The tenancies of six houses, lying between the High Market and the 'land of the Mother Church to Lincoln' (i.e. Stowe) in the South, were given to Hagin, son of Master Moses of London, almost certainly a relation of the executed Jews, on the payment of a 'fine'. This was the accepted procedure for escheated (re-possessed) property.

The house Hagin had chosen to live in was in Thorngate (South of the River near the 'Green Dragon'). When he died in 1280, no claims being made on his estate, this house was re-allocated by Edward to his clerk, William de Beverley.

Although no Jews would have openly remained in Lincoln by December 1290, Edward having ordered their expulsion from England in July, to be effected by November on pain of death, their substantial properties did. Three stone houses, all with possible Jewish associations may be seen on Steep Hill. On the West side stands 'The Jew's House' reputedly once owned by Bellaset of Wallingford, hanged for allegedly debasing the currency in 1200. Clipping coins had been one of Edward's complaints against the Jews. Either the Jews or the Saxon peasants were believed to be guilty. The latter were exonerated on the basis that they were too lacking in intelligence and skill!

'The Jews' Court', once believed to have been the setting for little St. Hugh's murder, is now the headquarters of the Society for Lincolnshire History and Archaeology. On the East side, at the corner of Christ's Hospital Road, another fine medieval building, once known as Aaron the Jew's house, but now as 'The Norman House' and dated c.1170 may be seen. A Jew of Northampton called Aaron and his heirs did hold two houses in Lincoln until 1227 when the property was granted to the Knights Templars. (Charter).

Eleanor had beneftted considerably from the wealth of the dis-possessed Jews.

The Bishops' Palace

Bishop Alexander had continued to live over the East Gate of the Roman City, but his successor, Bishop Robert Chesney, bought additional land from King Henry II between 1155 and 1158 and commenced building a residence in the

North-east corner of the Southern Extension. This Bishop's Palace, as it is now known, was quarried into the hillside, its East wall following a natural cleft in the rock which gave this first building a curious alignment, and relationship to the later additions.

This first palace consisted of two large areas, one above the other. The lower, which now appears like a cellar, was initially above ground level, as the windows demonstrate. There was also a range of buildings at the southern end.

The Two Hughs

Before 1290 the Palace had been much enlarged by work carried out under Bishop (St.) Hugh (1186-1200) and Bishop Hugh Wallys (of Wells, where he had been Archdeacon) 1209-1235. They were responsible for the hall on the West side with its purbeck marble pillars and central hearth, rooms above, and kitchens. The remains of these two halls, now administered by English Heritage are clearly labelled and worth visiting.

In 1290, the Palace must have been the most splendid residence in Lincoln, well suited to accommodate Kings and their immediate retinues. (*see fig. 10*)

10. The Bishop's Palace

The Franciscan Friary

Only one of Lincoln's five 1290 friaries lay within the walls. The grey Friary was situated in the south-west corner of the Southern Extension.

The story of the founding of this order by St. Francis of Assisi is well known. Franciscans came to England in 1224.

They were identified by the colour of their habits - then grey though now changed to brown - as Grey Friars, and also called the Friars Minors.

In Lincoln, the Order was given a house c.1230. Additional space was acquired when, in response to a request from King Henry III (1237) the men of Lincoln gave the Friars 'the place where pleas were held' - the ancient 'Geldehale'.

The Grey Friars' building programme included the blocking of the postern gate on the South wall of the Southern Extension, the enclosure of the lane which served it (1258) and the building of houses and a church 'on the wall'. The church was finished by 1268. This building 'on the wall' caused concern amongst the Citizens as it 'injured the City's defences'.

Part of this Friary survived. This was initially due to Robert Monson, the City Recorder, who established a free school in the remains in 1568 - recalled in the present Free School Lane. The school was renovated and now serves as The City and County Museum. These remains include a two naved, nine bay undercroft, the vaulted roof of which is supported by octagonal piers. Pevsner/Harris date it in the later 13th. century, after 1230. From their appearance, dating and position (built to the detriment of the Town's defences, just inside the Southern Extension wall the line of which is indicated by Broadgate) the remains are likely to have been part of the 1268 Friary church.

Speed places the 'Little Friars' (Friars Minors) outside the wall, North-east of Clasker Gate (O) which does not correlate with other evidence.

The Churches of Lincoln

At Domesday, five churches were recorded in Lincoln. Leland claimed 'I saw a roll wherein I counted there were thirty-eight parish churches in Lincoln City and the suburbs of it'. Defoe, nearly two hundred years later, found thirteen - 'the meanest to look on that are anywhere seen'. Such fluctuations are not only due to dramatic events, like the Reformation. In the past, as now, congregations shrank, churches failed, so were consequently abandoned or amalgamated.

Such fluidity, together with multiple dedications and gaps in documentary evidence, make a complete identification of all the parish churches viable in 1290 Lincoln and Wigford virtually impossible.

Hill Top Churches

In 1300, Hill (Medieval Lincoln) gives four churches

within the old Roman walls, St. Clement's, All Saints', St. Paul's and St. Mary Magdalene: and five just outside, St. Bartholomew on the West, St. Nicholas, Newport, St. Peter's and St. Leonard's both outside East Gate, and St. Margaret's, south-east of the Minster. Leland's '8 parish churches 'yet used for the North part on the Hill' probably includes churches outside the Roman walls. Speed shows St. Paul's, St. Margaret's, St. Peter's Eastgate and, at 'F' (St. Michael's) probably 'C' (omitted in key) St. Mary Magdalene.

St. Paul's

Of all the potential 1290 Hill-top churches, St. Paul's had the longest and most interesting history. Ordered by Paulinus, it had been built by his convert, Blaecca in 628 A.D. This church had already lost its roof 'by neglect or enemy damage' when recorded by Bede before 731 A.D. There was a St. Paul's of ancient foundation 'nearly all fallen down' in 1302, when Bishop Dalderby ordered its rebuilding. Bishop Dalderby's church was likely to have been that shown on Speed's map. St. Paul's was described by Stukeley, when he visited Lincoln in July, 1734. This building was demolished in 1786.

In 'The English Settlements' (Oxford) Myers writes:-

'Recent excavations on the site of the derelict church of St. Paul-in-the-Bail have shown that it probably overlay the remains of Paulinus' church. Conspicuously set in the first Christian building on the site, was a disturbed grave, which had been accompanied by a seventh-century enamelled hanging bowl, indicating a burial of a person of consequence, who might even have been Blaecca himself.'

The present church of St. Paul's was built 1877/8 by Sir A. Blomfield.

St. Peter in Eastgate

This church is also a Blomfield rebuild (1870) of an older foundation. A grant to maintain a chaplain at the 'Church of St. Peter in Eastgate' was made in 1285 (Patent). St. Peter's was damaged during the Civil War, when the Parliamentarian forces occupied the Hill-top, and demolished at the end of the 18th. century. A drawing of this church in a ruined state, by the early 18th. century engraver, Buck, survives.

St. Leonard's and All Saints'

A St. Leonard's is also mentioned in Eastgate in 1229. All Saints' was recorded in 1148 and 1321, suggesting that it would have been standing in 1290.

St. Mary Magdalene

This church was originally built between 1280 and 1299 in order to 'get parish services out of the West parts of the Cathedral' (Pevsner). There had been a long standing conflict between the pastoral and contemplative roles of the Christian clergy. Reformers believed the worldly contact, necessitated by the execution of pastoral duties, had a corrupting influence. The expulsion of the public from certain places of worship 'for the peace and ease of the clergy' was one of the results of this reform movement.

Ironically, at the Dissolution it was the use of religious buildings by parishioners, that saved them, wholly or in part, This is why Leland, Henry VIII's investigator, was so concerned to identify parish churches.

It is possible St. Mary Magdalene was not completely built in 1290.

The Churches of the Southern Extension

In 1290 the bulk of Lincoln's churches lay in the Southern Extension. Hill (Medieval Lincoln) identified 15 in 1300. In the Rolls parishes are used to identify property and so are themselves placed and identified. From the Rolls the parish of St. Michael on the Hill is shown to have included Parchmine Gate and to have lain opposite St. Andrews'. Both St. Martins and St. George's included 'Brantegate'. St. Martin's lay in the 'cloth market'. It had been given to the Cathedral by King William II ('Rufus'). (Charter January 6th. 1257). St. Swithen's was by Grey-friars and its parish included 'Stapleplace'. St. Cuthbert's was 'the most southerly parish'.

Inevitably, the trading area of a Town is volatile. The Southern Extension underwent much rebuilding in the 18th. and 19th. centuries and nothing of these churches appears to have survived.

THE SUBURBS

The Eastern Suburbs

The more Northerly of two Eastern suburbs described by Leland lay 'towards St. Beges, late a cell to St. Mary's Abbey, York'. Leland's reference to St. Beges has not been satisfactorily explained. The cell of St. Mary's York that lay in that vicinity was known as the Priory of St. Mary Magdalen.

The Priory of St. Mary Magdalen

This Priory was probably founded during the reign of Henry II (1154-1188) and was well established by 1260. Being a cell of York it was in charge of a Prior, subordinate to the Abbot.   The Prior in 1290 is not known but in 1297 it was John de Bryne (Patent).

Leland placed St. Beges - and therefore probably St. Mary Magdalen - 'scant ½ mile from the Minster'.   It is possible the Priory lands formed a wedge shape between the Roman road running from East Gate (Langworth Street/Gate - the present Wragby Road A158) and Greetwell Road.   The western point of this wedge would have been well within ½ mile of the Cathedral.   A spring at Greetwell, without the Suburb, lay on Priory land.   This would have taken the Eastern boundary well beyond Outer Circle Road.   Identifiable property held by the Priory at the Dissolution, (Dugdale 'Monasticum') suggests it extended Eastwards and that the wedge widened, bringing the Priory's eastern boundary nearer the River Witham.

This is probably why the well preserved remains standing in a recreation ground over a mile along Monk's Road are related to the Priory.   The most substantial part of these ruins has been identified (Cox, Pevsner/Harris) as the 'fairly complete' chancel of a chapel.   The Early English features which remain could place part of the building at the end of the 13th. century.

Although 'Mary Magdalen' appears in the key to Speed's map, (C) the Priory does not appear on the map itself.

The Dominican Friary

Speed does, however, show the Black Friars at 'N', outside the wall of The Southern Extension by Pottergate. The order of Dominican or Black Friars, also known as the Friars Preachers, was founded in Toulouse, by a Spanish nobleman, Dominic Guzman, recognised by Pope Honorius III in 1216 and introduced into England in 1221.   It swiftly became a prestigious order, renowned for its scholars and statesmen.

The Order was presided over by Provincials, each in charge of a Province.   Until the 15th. century, England, Ireland and Scotland constituted a single province, so the Dominican Provincials were men of some importance, often closely involved with Kings and affairs of state.   The enthronement of Robert Kilwarby, Provincial from 1261, as Archbishop of Canterbury was witnessed by Edward and probably Eleanor on their return to England after the Crusade.   Seventeen days later Robert was to crown Edward and Eleanor in Westminster Abbey Church.

William Hotham was twice Provincial (1282-7: 1290-6). In the interval between these two appointments when he was consigned to the Paris convent he refused to go pleading 'weighty affairs of State at the King's will'. He frequently acted as Edward's representative and was returning from a mission to the Pope when he died at Dijon aged 72. By Edward's command his corpse was embalmed, the viscera buried at Dijon and the body returned to England to be buried, with great pomp in the church of the Black Friars, London. (The Provincials of the Friars Preachers by The Rev. C.F.R. Palmer Archaeological Journal Vol.35).

The building programme of the Dominicans in Lincoln is indicated by grants of timber in 1238 and 1255. By 1260 they were ready to install a water system and obtained permission to enclose a spring belonging to the Priory of St. Mary Magdalen and pipe the water 'along the Highway' to their house. This building had a wooden tiled (shingled) roof, as wood, for what was probably a replacement, was granted in 1284. Their church was under construction May 1290 when timber was granted for the purpose. It was consecrated in 1311.

'Silvergate outside Pottergate' was given as the early site of the Friary (V.C.H.) which corresponds with the position on Speed's map. Inevitably the Friary expanded, receiving in 1284 a messuage and garden in Lincoln from the Harby landowner, John Cotty, together with 3 other small messuages and a plot of land 20 foot broad adjoining 'for the enlargement of their place'. In 1285 they were allowed to enclose a piece of land 125 foot square on their North side. By the Dissolution the site extended to c.10 acres.

The Friars of the Penance of Jesus Christ

The House of the friars of the Penance of Jesus Christ was established south-west of the Black Friars and Clasker Gate, on the North side of the River Witham, before 1266 when Henry III granted them a 'vacant place adjoining their houses'. Members of this order were popularly known as the Friars of the Sack, possibly a reference to their wearing sackcloth. In a will of 1323 their Lincoln house was referred to as sekfreres (Hill).

By the second Council of Lyons (1274) all mendicant orders, except the Dominicans, Franciscans, Augustins and Carmelites, were suppressed. The Sack Friars, covered by this order, were not allowed to accept new members. Their Lincoln house was probably failing by 1307, when the Abbot of Barlings tried to acquire the site (Hill).

Thorngate was particularly associated with the Kyme family who held property there. An inquisition held in 1312 established a messuage in Thornbridge Gate, formally inhabited by the Sack Friars, as the property of Philip de

Kyme (I.P.M.). In 1357 Joan, who had been married to a William de Kyme, and then to Nicholas de Cantilupe, was allowed to found a chantry of five chaplains dedicated to St. Peter for her second husband on the Friary site 'in the suburb of Lincoln'.

Edward and Eleanor and the Sack Friars

Dugdale (Monasticum) claimed Queen Eleanor 'took the Friars of the Sack in London under her protection'. It is not clear whether he was referring to Eleanor of Castile or Edward's mother. However, money was given to the Sack Friars by Eleanor of Castile's executors 'for the soul of the Queen'.

On Edward's death in 1307 a chantry of 3 priests was established at Reepham church, north-east of Lincoln, which was held by the Sack Friars. On the failure of the house this church and chantry were taken over by the Vicars of Lincoln Cathedral.

The Suburb of Wigford

The most substantial of Lincoln's suburbs lay South of the River Witham, stretching along both sides of Ermine Street, towards London. It was known as Wigford or Wickenford, a name suggesting an Angle settlement at a place where the River had been fordable.

Water and Bridges

Leland 'heard say' that the lower part of the Town (called Wickerford) was all marsh and won by policy. Sincil Dike, the Gowts Drain and near right-angled turn south by the River Witham through Bradeford, manifest such 'policy' - an early manipulation of the natural water system for trade, or defence against attack or flood.

Sincil Dike, which ran South from the Eastern arm of the Witham protected Ermine Street and its ribbon development on the East; the River protected it along the West. These two waterways were joined by a drain called Gotes or Gowts, shown dividing into two arms on Speed's map. At the junction of this drain with Sincil Dike, Hill identified a pool known as Nicorpool, 'Nicor' being Old English for a water monster.

Of the six bridges shown by Speed, three carry Ermine Street through Wigford on its way to London.

High Bridge

The River Witham was crossed by the Great Bridge (Pons Magna 1146) called High Bridge by Leland and so identified today. Cox dated the stone barrel vaulting, the oldest part of the present bridge, c.1235, suggesting the Bridge had been extended eastwards to support the rebuilt and enlarged chapels. Leland noted a bridge chapel dedicated to St. George and Hill one dedicated to St. Thomas Becket. The present Bridge encompasses a further extension, on the West side, to support the half-timbered houses there, dating from c.1540.

Goats' Bridge

Goat's (Gotes, Gowt's etc.) Drain was and is crossed by Goat's Bridges. Hill gives a 1275 reference to 'Ponts de Gotes'. A two-arched bridge is shown on Speed's map.

The Bargates

At the extreme South end of Wigford Speed shows a limited wall and two gate defence. Hill considers this the subject for a repair order made in 1228 (Liberate Rolls). The road to Canwick left by the more easterly of the two gates, known as East or Little Bargate. Ermine Street continued through Great or West Bargate to cross Sincil Dike, which curved West to meet the River Witham, by Great Bargate Bridge.

Sketches of both gates were made by Buck in the 18th. century and are reproduced in Hill. That of West Bargate shows the less impressive structure, suggesting this gate may have been by then rebuilt. It was demolished mid 18th. century. Little Bargate survived to feature in Peter de Wint's painting 'Lincoln from the South' (Usher Gallery) but was destroyed shortly afterwards.

Wigford Churches in 1290

Leland mentions eleven churches in Wigford, one in 'clear ruins' Hill lists twelve for the 13th. century, five on the east side of Ermine Street and seven on the West. Of these early churches three survive, St. Benedict's on the West and St. Mary-le-Wigford and St. Peter at Gowts on the East.

St. Benedict's

This church, just South of High Bridge was given by Henry II to Robert Bloet, Bishop of Lincoln between 1100 and 1123. It was patched up after extensive damage suffered during the 17th. century Civil War.

Mary-le-Wigford

St. Mary's stands on the corner of St. Mary Street and Hugh Street. It incorporates some Saxon elements, though the body of the church was built c.1263.

St. Peter at Gowts

It is claimed this Church was not always identified as 'at Gowts' so it probably acquired this name from Gotes

Bridge near which it stands. Aisles were added during the 12th. and 13th. centuries. It was substantially restored in the 19th. century, but some Saxon and Norman parts remain.

Two of the lost churches have 20th. century remembrancers. St. Marks, mentioned in 1249, was recalled in St. Mark's Railway Station now closed; it is still remembered in St. Mark's Street, on the West side of High Street (Ermine Street). A 19th. century St. Mark's church which had replaced the medieval building was, in its turn demolished and the parish finally amalgamated with that of St. Mary-le-Wigford. A modern church of St. Andrew's replaced the older foundation (recorded 1257).

The remaining 13th. century Wigford churches given by Hill are, on the West, St. John, St. Edward's, Holy Cross and St. Margaret's; on the East, the well-documented Holy Trinity, St. Michael's and St. Botolph's.

The Carmelite Friary

Leland placed the White Friars on the west side of Wigford High Street. The Friary lay between the churches of St. Mark and St. Edward, traditionally on the site of St. Mark's Station, i.e. between St. Mark Street and Firth Road.

Hermits from Mount Carmel received a primitive rule c.1210, and papal recognition as an order in 1226. As the Crusaders lost the Holy Land, these hermits fled first to Cyprus and then to Europe. They arrived in England, settling at Alnwick c.1246. In the following year a new rule was approved and the hermits lived together as mendicant friars. The wearing of a white mantle over a brown habit gave them the name of White Friars. The Order was under the protection of the Virgin Mary.

The founder of the Carmelite Friary in Wigford was, according to Speed, Odo de Kilkenny, a Scot. Leland names the Scottish founder as Gualterus (Walter) Dorotheus. Leland's candidate has not been identified. His notes were subjected to much misuse before they were published by Hearne in the 18th. century and what he originally wrote may have been distorted. He does, however, support Speed's claim that the founder was a Scot.

Speed's 'Kilkenny' opens a more promising line of enquiry. Both the Irish town of that name and the County, with at least three Carmelite convents, were in existence prior to the founding of the Lincoln Carmelite house. Indeed a William de Kilkenny had been Bishop of Ely, but in 1255/6 thirteen years before the Lincoln Carmelites were known to exist. The references to a Scottish founder do not exclude an Irish connection as the Scots originated in Ireland.

'St. Mary's Gildhall'

On the other side of High Street (Ermine Street) just North of St. Peter at Gowts, stands a building known as 'John O' Gaunt's Stables', 'St. Mary's Gildhall', and called by Leland 'the Gildhall 'longing to St. Anne's Church of the foundation of the Burton and Sutton merchants'. The building which dates from the 12th. century, has undergone additions, decay, demolitions and changes in use.

11. St. Mary's Gildhall

The earlier history of the 'Gildhall' can only be surmised. The great doorway decoration (*see fig. 11*) slit window, and wall of the High Street frontage all suggest a substantial building. It is possible the original structure was higher (Cox). Although Margaret Wood identifies the mutilated heads as those of bishops, she classifies the building as domestic, not ecclesiastical architecture, as did Professor Hamilton Thompson. The doorway is similar to that of the 12th. century keep door at Berkeley Castle.

The builder of such an establishment must have been a man of some standing, and, as recent excavations have uncovered a rutted road beneath the foundations, one able to obstruct a used road with impunity. Perhaps a Gaunt (Gant or Ghent) association is not impossible but with Gilbert, friend to King Stephen, briefly Earl of Lincoln who died c.1156, rather than the great 14th. century John. The transference of the Earldom suggests Gilbert had no surviving children. By feudal law, in the event of there being no heirs, property returned (escheated) to the Crown.

The second function of this building was to house the Gild of St. Mary. How the transfer from a private dwelling was effected is not certain. It may have been in the following way. In 1237 the 'men of Lincoln' lost their public building the 'Hall of Pleas' when, at King Henry's request, they had donated it to the Grey Friars. Some form of compensation could reasonably be expected and this may have come in the form of the 'Gant' property, serving a double purpose as Hall of Pleas and Gildhall. In 1272 the Hall of Pleas was identified as 'Geldehale'. (Charter Rolls).

The deal probably took place in 1250. In that year Michael de la Burne, the King's Butler, was provided with a messuage in the City of Lincoln. He then, with the King's approval, made over 'land and buildings' lying between the High Street and Sincil Dike in the parish of St. Andrew Wigford, which he had held of the King, to the Gild of St. Mary. As the situation given for this property matches with that of the surviving St. Mary's Gildhall, the 'land and buildings' could have been the 'Gant' house, which, having reverted to the Crown, had been granted to various tenants, the last being Michael de la Burne. This being the case, it would have been functioning as St. Mary's Gildhall in 1290.

Later History

By some means the Gildhall, although associated with a religious gild, survived the Dissolution and came into the hands of the Town Council. In 1664, being in a state of decay, 'Mary Hall' was leased to Edward Fawks, who may have built up a wall, using 'Norman stones two-shafted windows and a buttress'.

Daniel Defoe, visiting Lincoln in the early 18th. century, found it so full of the 'ruins of monasteries and religious houses that the vary barns, stables out-houses, and, as they showed me, some of the very hog-sties were built church fashion'. It is not impossible that, at this time, the Gildhall was used for stabling and, John of Gaunt being in vogue, perhaps aided by the memory of Gilbert Gaunt, acquired the name 'John O' Gaunt's Stables'.

57

During the 19th. century the wings were divided up and used by various traders. In the 1930's the Gildhall was bought by public subscription and Lincoln Corporation. It is in use as St. Peter at Gowt's church hall, but undergoing restoration. It is hoped that the ancient road with its wheel marks will remain open to view.

Gilds

The word 'Gild' can be related to two anglo-saxon words - 'geld/gild' meaning an association and 'gelden/gyldan' meaning to pay. In England, a gild reference is found in the laws of Ine, King of Wessex, before 726 A.D. It refers to a society, Gegildan, formed by thanes to aid in payments of wergeld (bloodmoney), virtually, an insurance company. A continental reference is clarified in 884, when villeins were forbidden to form a defensive associations 'vulgarly called gilds'; suggesting an organization akin to a trade union.

In the second half of the 11th. century and during the 12th. century, gilds re-emerged as trade associations. As early medieval craftsmen tended to market their own goods, it is difficult to separate these into merchant and craft gilds. Statutes survive for 11th. century associations in Cambridge, Abbotsbury and Exeter. The London Weavers' Gild claimed a charter from Henry I (1100-1135). In Lincoln, the weavers, who gained a charter from Henry II (1154-1189) formed The Gild of the Holy Cross.

The main concern of most early gild members was to establish a local trade monopoly. A fixed annual sum was paid to the Crown in return for a charter giving gild members exclusive trading rights. Inevitably, non-members objected. Both the London and Lincoln weavers' gilds experienced opposition.

However, the Gild movement gained strength. A government inquiry held in 1389 revealed there were, by then, gilds in most English towns. They were again changing their nature. The religious concern incorporated in the early statutes of Abbotsbury and Exeter had flourished and the religious gild, with merchant, aristocratic, and Court membership, social functions, charitable and educational enterprises, emerging as a prestigious and powerful entity. Such was the Gild of St. Mary in Wigford. Though not the Gild of St. Anne, it could well have been 'of the foundation of Burton and Sutton merchants' as Leland claimed.

As well as the Gilds of the Holy Cross and St. Mary, Lincoln did have a Gild of St. Anne and a more unusual Gild of St. Edmund of Potigny, established in 1276. St. Edmund (Rich) had been a friend of Lincoln's Bishop Grosseteste. Edward's cousin, Edmund, had been named after him.

Without Great Bargate

Outside the main gate of Wigford stood two important buildings, on the right (West) the Priory of St. Catherine and on the left (East) The Hospital of the Holy Innocents.

St. Catherine's Priory

The Priory was of the local order of Gilbert of Sempringham, the only English order founded in the Middle Ages. Gilbert was the son of a Norman knight who had held the lordship of Sempringham, a manor in the Lincolnshire fens. Considered so sickly he was excused knight service, Gilbert is reputed to have lived for a hundred years. (c.1089-1189).

The beginnings of the Order were slight. A convent of nuns was established at Sempringham. Lay brothers were recruited to act as bailiffs and provide manual labour. In 1147 Gilbert failed to incorporate his order with the Cistercians, but the following year it received papal recognition, and Bishop Robert Chesney of Lincoln founded St. Catherine's Priory, outside Wigford.

The introduction of regular canons resulted in a rebellion by the lay brothers in 1166/7. The leaders complained to the Papal Curia at Sens, alleging sexual misconduct in the Gilbertine convents, and Gilbert was ordered to house the canons and nuns in completely separate establishments. A double monastery being an essential feature of his Order, Gilbert contested this decree. He was supported by five bishops and by the King, Henry II, who threatened to withdraw all the Order's endowments if it were altered in any way.

(The Revolt of the Lay Brothers of Sempringham English History Review No. 50 by M.D. Knowles).

The double monasteries continued with men and women occupying separate buildings, usually on either side of the conventual church. In the church the two communities were divided by a screen and communion was passed through a carefully supervised turn-stile. The sexes met at the general chapters held at Sempringham, but the nuns were required to travel in enclosed carts. Three prioresses took turns to control the nuns' affairs. (Medieval Monasticism - Lawrence).

St. Catherine's Priory must have been a substantial religious house. Not only had Bishop Chesney a reputation for extravagant building but, at the Dissolution, Henry VIII found it a suitable gift for his brother-in-law, Charles Brandon. There was a 'great church' in 1255, for the high altar of which Henry III gave a silver-gilt cup. In 1285 the

'Prior and convent were granted a licence to build a windmill 'east of the Priory gate'.

By the 19th. century the Priory had disappeared but, in 1876, a new road and housing development led to the discovery of coffins and stone remnants by which the Rev. Veneables was able to situate the Priory 'just outside the south city gate, at the junction of Ermine and Fosse Way'. Leland had placed it 'on the south-west side of Barre Gate' which would correspond. To-day this area is known as St. Catherine's.

The Hospital of Holy Innocents

Outside Barre Gate on the south-east side, nearly opposite St. Catherine's, stood the hospital for lepers known as La Malanderie. Dugdale names Remigius, the first Bishop of Lincoln, as its founder, but, in a Patent Roll for 1284, it was claimed to have been founded by 'former Kings of England'.

In that year, the Sheriff was ordered to take charge of the Hospital, probably because of some laxity as it was decreed that two chaplains should reside with the brothers in one house and that the lepers and sisters - presumably nursing nuns - live separately. In 1290 Andrew Fraunceys of Maltby was appointed chaplain, but only on probation, the House having suffered 'carelessness under former keepers' (Patent).

Admissions

There seems to have been some competition to gain places at the Hospital. The lepers were restricted to twelve, new inmates being appointed only when a vacancy occurred. When a Dionisia de Retford gained a place as a sister at Holy Innocents this was referred to as an 'exhibition' suggesting something of an award. Later, in the reign of Edward III, an inquisition discovered a woman had gained admission by a bribe given to the 'Custos'. Perhaps the House's attraction was partly due to its royal patronage. At the Clipstone Parliament one of Edward's acts was to order the admission of William le Forester, a leper, to 'his house of lepers without Lincoln.' (Patent).

Two Women at Holy Innocents

Margaret, the widow of Alan Everard of Burgh by Weynflet, became a resident at Holy Innocents in an unusual way. Hanged for having harboured her son Robert, who had been accused of theft, her body was brought back to the Hospital for burial. There she 'drew breath and revived' remaining for two years or more, as an inmate, before

Edward pardoned her in 1284, because 'her recovery is ascribed to a miracle'. (Patent).

Iveyt de Rouceby was buried at Holy Innocents. Her elaborate sepulchral slab with its inscription in the Court language of Norman French suggests a woman of some standing. It has been dated 1350 but could be earlier.

The discovery of this slab, during the laying of a railway line (now dismantled) between Honington and Lincoln Central Station, in 1865, has verified the siting of Holy Innocents in the north-west corner of South Common. The area is still called Malandry Closes, (fields). According to Edward Trollope the Hospital site was marked on several local maps and the remains of the original buildings were destroyed by fire in the middle of the 18th. century.

The Cortège in Lincoln

This was the Lincoln to which the Cortège came, the Queen's body preceeded by Robert of St. Alban's, on horseback and bearing a cross. It arrived on or after November 29th. and departed on December 4th. In the interim, the Queen's body was embalmed and the viscera buried in the Angel Choir of the Cathedral.

Medieval Embalming

During the Middle Ages, the bodies of saints, potential saints, royalty and even important royal servants, might have to undergo long journeys to the places appointed for their burials. In death, as in life, the great had to be suitably housed, hence Eleanor's journey to Westminster. The shrines of saints brought prestige and income to the religious establishments which housed them. A saint who died away from his or her convent or cathedral, such as Bishop (St.) Hugh of Lincoln, would be brought back, regardless of distance.

Though embalming fulfilled a practical need and was practised in Court and religious circles, it is rarely mentioned. Possibly, the Church felt its pagan ritualistic associations made it an undesirable, though necessary, practice. Also, the reverence and wonder aroused by the uncorrupted bodies of the exhumed Kings and Saints could have been diminished if the processes by which this had been achieved were widely known!

The Queen's Embalming

Clues to the method by which the Queen's body was preserved are found in her wardrobe accounts for 1290. Payment was recorded for a bushel (8 gallons) of barley 'to place in the Queen's body' a pound of incense, and 6 ells (c.7½ yards) of cloth 'in which to wrap the body'. It would appear the barley was to replace the bulk, lost by the removal of the heart and viscera, which were both given separate burials.

When the body arrived at Westminster Abbey Church it was in a coffin 'full of spices'. (Westminster Abbey Official Guide).

The place and perpetrators of the Queen's embalming are not known, but circumstantial evidence favours the Dominican Friary and the Black Friars, particularly if the Cortège entered by the North Gate. The Friary was equipped with a water supply in 1290, probably the only Lincoln establishment to enjoy this sophistication. It was reasonably convenient to the Cathedral, lying in the vicinity of Pottergate. The embalming of William Hotham, not six years later, showed the Black Friars were accustomed to embalming in this fashion. There were close associations between the Dominicans and the Court, Eleanor's heart being buried at Black Friars, London.

The Vigil

It was customary for the bodies of important people to lie before the high Altar of a convent church or a cathedral. The procedure for the reception and vigil accorded to St. Hugh at Lincoln Cathedral (Minster) in 1220 has been outlined by Hoveden. King John together with his Earls and Barons met the cortège and carried the body to the porch of the Cathedral, where it was received by the Archbishop and bishops. It was then carried on the shoulders of the priests into the choir where it remained overnight, the service for the dead being performed about it. Queen Eleanor's body was probably afforded the same rites.

A Scenario

If the Cortège entered the North Gate; the Queen's body were embalmed at the Dominican Friary; returned by way of Pottergate to the Cathedral (a difficult path before Lindum Road was built - but, lying diagonally across the gradient, not as difficult as Steep Hill); the King and main Court officers housed in the Bishop's Palace and, after the funeral the Cortège left by way of Pottergate, re-entering the Southern Extension by Claskergate and, again crossing the gradient diagonally to the South Gate (now Stonebow) they could have crossed the River Witham by the Great (High) Bridge and, regaining Ermine Street, passed through Wigford and out by Barre Gate. There, the cross site could have been selected and the Cortège continue along Ermine Street towards Grantham.

There is no substantial evidence for this scenario, but St. Catherine's Priory, suggested by W. Stevenson in 'The Death of Queen Eleanor of Castile in Nottinghamshire' far from the Cathedral and administrative centre, outside even the scanty defences of Wigford, has less to recommend it as the place of Eleanor's embalming and overnight vigil and Court entertainment.

The Queen's Monuments

The Tomb at Lincoln Cathedral

Eleanor's tomb was destroyed by the 17th. century iconoclasts, but two records of it have survived. 'In Our Lady's Chapel, at the East end of the North side of the Church, is buried the bowels of Queen Eleanor. The arms of Castile be on the side of the tomb, ' wrote Leland. Anticipating the destruction, Sir Christopher Hatton commissioned Sir William Dugdale, the 17th. century herald and Warwickshire historian, and William Sedwick, heraldic draughtsman, to record certain memorials. At Lincoln, drawings were made of the shields depicted in the great East window of the Lady Chapel, and of Eleanor's tomb. As well as four shields on the side of the altar tomb, Castile quatering Leon at the ends, enclosing Ponthieu and England in the middle panels, the drawing shows the Queen's effigy and the inscription round the verge.

In the accounts the first of three payments for this tomb appears towards the end of 1291. A part payment of £5 was made to Dymenge de Leger and Alexander of Abingdon (later called the Image-maker) for 'making the tomb above the Queen's viscera at Lincoln'. They received a further £6.13s.4d in the following Spring. In the final payment of the £20 fee (£8.6s.8d) the tomb is described as 'of marble'. In 1293, Roger Crundale, who finished the work on the cross at Charing (see London to Westminster. Chapter XI) was paid £1.16s.8d for marble and operations around the viscera of the Queen'.

The Queen's Images

Only one payment is made to William Torel, the maker of the other two large images, for the image on this tomb. He received £2 after Easter 1292. The large tomb images are discussed more fully under Westminster, where the only original survives.

Alexander the Image-maker was paid £4.6s.8d for making three small images of wax for the tombs of Lincoln and Black Friars, London. These were cast in metal by William Suffolk of London, for which he received £5.6s.8d.

The Re-created Tomb at Lincoln

The present tomb in the Angel Choir at Lincoln Cathedral is a 19th. century recreation in which it has been assumed the large image was identical with that at Westminster Abbey Church. In both, and in the Dugdale-Sedgwick drawing the Queen is shown holding the string of her cloak, as she is in her seal (*see figs. 12 & 13*) and cross statues. At Lincoln she holds a sceptre, not present in the drawing or at Westminster.

The drawing is roughly executed but some differences are firmly stated. The image hood is shorter, the Queen's hair is straighter and longer, there is no sceptre and the right hand appears to lie flat.

12. The Queen's Seal

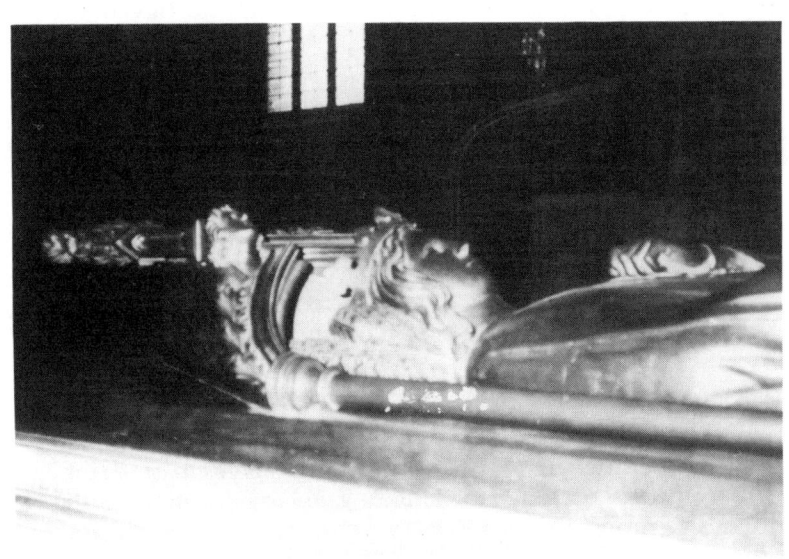

13. The Image from the Re-created Tomb

The Queen's Cross

Though first on the route, the Lincoln cross is the second to be recorded in the Accounts of the Queen's Executors. The first payment was made during the Michaelmas (Autumn) Term, 1290: the last payment between Whitsun and the Autumn of 1292. Richard of Stowe, cementarius, (architect/stone-mason) received four payments of £20 each, one payment of 20 marks and two of 10 marks for this cross, the total being £106.13s.4d.

Robert of Corfe was paid 7 marks (£4.13s.4d.) for 3 rods, rings and hoods for the crosses at Waltham, Northampton and Lincoln, during the Michaelmas Term 1291. If this part-payment were divided equally amongst the three crosses £1.11s.1.1/3d. would have been added to the cost of the Lincoln Cross. William de Hiberna, first described as an image-maker and later 'cementarius', was contracted to make and carry rods, hoods and rings for the Lincolnshire cross, towards the end of 1291, for 22 marks. The final payment, lumped together with one for work on Northampton Cross was made in Hilary Term 1292. This would have placed the total cost of the Lincoln cross at £122.17s.9.1/3d. without images. The provision of rods, rings and hoods, and the surviving fragment prove the cross bore statues of the Queen. These appear to have been mass produced by Alexander the image-maker and William de Hiberna at a cost of £3.6s.8d. each. The numbers of statues on the crosses varied, the lowest known being three (Geddington) so the images would add at least £10 to the total cost of the Lincoln cross.

14. The Cross Site

Hill gives references for the Cross in 1389 when gild members, going on pilgrimages, were to be escorted to and from the Queen's Cross (Gild certificates): for 1445/6 when the citizens were ordered to meet King Henry VI at the 'cross on the cliff' and in 1568 when Edmund Yarburgh was accused of feeding sheep on the city commons 'between the Queen's Cross and the common ground of the City'. (C.C.M.)

15. Fragment of the Lincoln Cross

Leland sited the Lincoln cross 1534-42 in the suburb without the Barre Gate by South of the Town which stretched towards Bracebridge.

'(A little) without Barre is a very fair (cross) and large.' (Itinerary). Unfortunately the words in brackets were supplied by Herne, being illegible in the m.s.

On the basis of this evidence the cross is believed to have stood outside Wigford by St. Catherine's Priory at the old junction of Ermine Street with the Fosse Way, near the present Cross O' Cliff Hill. (*see fig. 14*)

It had disappeared by the early 18th. century. However a fragment, the skirt of one of the Queen's images, was recovered in the 19th. century, and may now be seen in the Castle grounds. (*see fig. 15*). It had been used as a footbridge across a dyke.

PART III

Grantham

Lincoln to Grantham

The possibility of the Court's travelling to Grantham by the River Witham cannot be totally dismissed, but, if the River followed its present winding course, such a journey would have had to cover c. 34 miles against the current. With time consumed by loading and unloading this would make the journey impossible to execute in a single day of limited daylight under anything other than the most propitious conditions, so it is more likely that the Cortège travelled by land.

By Land to Ancaster

The land route lay along Ermine Street, which continued from Wigford through the Domesday settlement of Bracebridge, across the Heaths, by Navenby, past the Preceptory of Temple Bruer to Ancaster. This was the most direct way available from Lincoln to London and one favoured by Medieval Kings (see 'Medieval Roads' Brian Hindle Shire Archaeology Series)

To-day, the old Ermine Street has been truncated for the airfield at Waddington, but the remainder, surviving as 'The Viking Way' and 'High Dike', may be reached from the present Lincoln-Grantham Road (A607) c.4½ miles South of Wigford by the B1178 East from Harmston. Leland accurately reported this journey, from Lincoln (Wigford) to Ancaster '16 miles all by plain ground'.

En Route

Along the West side of this stretch of Ermine Street lay seven Domesday manors, Bracebridge, Waddington, Harmston, Coleby, Boothby Graffoe, Navenby and Wellingore. For all except Navenby, priests and churches were recorded in the 'Domesday' book. There remains some physical evidence of pre-1290 churches in all except Boothby Graffoe. As the last has survived as a settlement it may be assumed all these manors were in existence when the Cortège passed.

Seven 1290 Churches

Apart from the 19th. century North aisle, transept and

chapel, All Saints, BRACEBRIDGE is substantially Anglo-Saxon. Pevsner/Harris note a Norman 'tub' font and an 11th. century tower.

The church at WADDINGTON was destroyed during the Second World War. One 'stiff-leaf' (Early English type of decorative foliage) capital from the early church has survived.

HARMSTON All Saints' has Norman elements and is likely to be later than All Saints', COLEBY, wherein Saxon contributions are identified by Pevsner/Harris.

St. Andrew's, BOOTHBY GRAFFOE is an 1842 re-build. Although St. Peter's NAVENBY was substantially re-built in the 18th. and 19th. centuries, some late 13th. century work is identified by Pevsner/Harris.

The oldest part of the church at WELLINGORE, the fourth to be dedicated to All Saints', is a 12th. century sedilia (priests' seats) on the South side of the chancel. At Domesday, this church was held by St. Peter's, Lincoln.

Temple Bruer

On the East side of Ermine Street, at the South end of Wellingore Heath, 12 miles from Wigford and roughly half way to Grantham, stood the great Preceptory of Temple Bruer. This establishment of the Knights Templars had been founded before 1195, when the Knights were granted a market and a church. The latter was constructed in the Eastern style, popular with the military orders. Leland noted the East end of the Temple 'is made 'opere circulari de more' ' and was struck by the 'great and vast buildings'. Some of the ruins stand to-day.

No record of a 1290 visit to the Preceptory has emerged, though it would have been well situated to provide rest and provisions for the Cortège; and the Court were probably housed there on another occasion. King Henry VIII is reputed to have stayed there with his fifth wife, Katherine Howard.

Ancaster

At Byard's Leap, just under 3 miles south-west of Temple Bruer, Ermine Street is crossed by the A17 and it becomes the B6403. It runs through Ancaster (identified as the Roman station Causennae of the Antonine Itinerary) as the town's main North-South thoroughfare.

Ancaster was a walled town and some stretches of the wall and ditch remain. Otherwise, only the church of St. Martin has survived from the 13th. century. Quarries, about two miles from Ancaster provided building stone for Lincolnshire during the Medieval period.

Ancaster to Grantham

The Lincolnshire Cliff or Edge, a ridge running through the County from the Humber to Grantham, at times 400 feet high, is here known as High Dike. After Ancaster, Ermine Street continues along High Dike, passing 3 miles East of Grantham. To enter Grantham it was, therefore, necessary to leave Ermine Street and cross the River Witham.

To-day there are two roads from High Dike which join to enter the northern part of Grantham by Manthorpe Road. These routes are served by different bridges, shown on Armstrong's map of 1779. They both pass through Domesday manors, linking them with Ermine Street and Grantham, so are likely to have been in use in 1290.

The first route, now interrupted by an airfield, left Ermine Street c.¾ mile South of Ancaster, traversing Barkston Heath diagonally to cross the River Witham at Belton. In this Domesday manor medieval remains are found only in the 'badly over restored' church of St. Peter and St. Paul, where Pevsner/Harris date the lower part of the West tower c.1200. At Belton the road joins the A607, which runs through Manthorpe a 19th. century estate village and so enters Grantham.

Leaving Ermine Street c. 3½ miles South of Ancaster, the second route passes through the Domesday manor of Londonthorpe. Here, the early heritage, preserved in the church of St. John the Baptist, is more substantial than that found at Belton. According to Pevsner/Harris it includes an early 13th. century South arcade, a North arcade of c.1300, possibly under construction in 1290, and (in the North Aisle) a cross-legged (crusader) tomb and a fragmentary 13th. century coffin lid with a foliated cross. From Longthorpe the route now skirts Belton Park, then turns South-west crossing the River Witham by the Town Bridge - a medieval bridge survived here until the beginning of this century - to join the A607 (Manthorpe Road).

On the basis of current evidence it would be impossible to advantage either route. The terrain through which both roads passed was likely to have been wooded. The distances to be covered, even considering route did not in 1290 have to divert for Belton Park, were approximately the same (c. 6 miles). The second route would have given the Cortège a longer stretch on the highroad but, having once left Ermine Street, it would have been faced with more severe gradients. Any assumption that the town bridge was kept in better repair would depend in the first instance on the Knights Templars from Temple Bruer's not using the Belton bridge when visiting their Grantham property. Whichever route the Cortège followed it would have entered Grantham the same way, as is shown on the main route map.

The Manor and Soke of Grantham

At Domesday, Grantham, a vill on the River Witham, possessed a manorial hall, a church dedicated to St. Wulfram, a chapel given by the nun, Alswith, to the monastery of St. Peter's at Burgh, 4 mills, and 7 gardens.

Essentially a market town, Grantham was never walled. It expanded as a ribbon development along the Medieval Great North Road, which came from Newark (now the A1) entered the settlement as the present B1174 and, running roughly parallel to the River, served as the Town's main thoroughfare.

Grantham would have provided a useful stopping place for travellers from both Newark and Lincoln, but there was no monastic house to accommodate them. This need was filled by the Knights Templars, who built an inn, opposite Grantham's market place on the High Street/Great North Road, before 1213. It became known as 'The Angel'.

It would appear Grantham had the right to hold a market before this date, although no charter specifically naming the settlement in this respect has emerged. It is not impossible that the Templars held the market they were granted in 1195, in Grantham, rather than in Temple Bruer, which was a more remote site. This may explain later conflicts over the Market Square which arose between the townspeople and Lord of the Manor.

In 1253/4 the manorial residence was designated a 'castle'. Before 1290 the Franciscan friars were established behind the market place in the vicinity of the present Greyfriars and it is possible the number of mills was reduced to three.

Ladies and Lords of the Manor

Some of the confusion over the early ownership of the manor of Grantham stems from the two-tier system of possession operating under the Norman and Angevin Kings. By this, property remained in the King's hands, being leased to tenants-in-chief, at first in return for military service, but, by the 13th. century, a cash alternative was allowed. Eventually, the tenants assumed the rights of ownership, though this was not officially acknowledged until the 17th. century. At the death or defection of the tenant the property was re-possessed (escheated) by the Ruler. It was usually re-allocated to the mature heir on the payment of a 'fine'.

Certain manors tended to be granted in dower, to provide the Queen, Queen Dowager, the tenant's wife or widow, with an income. Between 1066 and 1290 Grantham had formed part of the dower of four Queens. Before Domesday it had been the property of Edith the widow of King Edward the Confessor. When she died in 1075/6 it came to William the Conqueror's Queen, Matilda, who, on her death in 1083 left all her English properties to her youngest son, Henry. He was kept from his inheritance until he became King in 1100.

Henry was survived by his second wife, Adeliza. She was granted Arundel Castle and married William d'Albini, the King's butler, who was created Count of Arundel. The line failed in 1242/3 (Knights' Fees). In an inquest to discover the true heir it was declared that the Countess of Arundel *had* held Grantham. It would appear the manor had passed from Henry through Adeliza to the Albinis of Arundel.

However, in an inquest of 1237, it had been declared that the Earl of Warenne and Surrey held Grantham with the Soke (right of jurisdiction) 'of the gift of King John' (1199-1216). This apparent conflict of ownership may be explained by the descent of the Warenne family.

The third William Warenne was one of those Earls who had deserted King Stephen at the 'Joust of Lincoln'. He died on a crusade 7 years later leaving an only child, Isabel, to inherit his estates.

Isabel married King Stephen's younger son, William. By the Treaty of Wallingford, made between Stephen and Duke Henry in 1153, Henry was to become King of England after Stephen's death and William was to keep his own and his wife's estates in England and France and the Earldom of Warenne and Surrey. Stephen died the following year and William four years later, without issue.

Henry II re-possessed William's estates, but returned them in 1163 on Isabel's marriage to his half brother, Hamelin, an illegitimate son of Geoffrey of Anjou. Isabel died in 1199 and Hamelin in 1202.

King John escheated the estates but returned the Norman property to William, Isabel and Hamelin's son and heir. William had married Maud, a grand-daughter of William d'Albini and Adeliza. She would have brought English property as a dowry, probably including Grantham and Stamford. In 1204 Normandy and all the lands there of the Anglo-norman barons were lost. King John granted William the Warenne English properties 'until he should regain his French possessions'. It is likely this confirmation of English property by King John included Maud's dower, and that this was the document being quoted in 1237. As Maud died childless Grantham passed to the Warenne family, who held it as tenants-in-chief.

William made a second advantageous marriage to another Maud, one of the five daughters and heiresses of Anselm Marshal (the Earl of Pembroke) and widow of the Earl of Norfolk. By this Maud William had a son, John, who succeeded him and a daughter, Isabel, who married the Earl of Arundel.

John was still a minor (under 21) when he married in 1247. He must have attained his majority the following year when he was summoned to Council, and so was probably born in 1227. He had married Alice, the half sister of King Henry III and supported the King and Lord Edward against Simon de Montfort and the barons. After the Battle of Lewes, John's main property, he fled abroad, returning to fight against Earl Simon at Evesham.

Dugdale (Baronage) tells two stories about this John of Warenne. In 1269 he was involved in a violent dispute with Sir Alan le Zouche and his son. All three were summoned to Westminster to settle their differences, but John assaulted his opponents and then fled to his castle at Reigate, pursued by the Lord Edward. John submitted and was fined 10,000 marks, a substantial sum, to be paid off at the rate of 200 marks a year, by which time he would probably have been 92.

The 'Quo Warranto' Legend

In 1277 the tenants-in-chief were required to justify their rights to their tenancies. The investigation became known by the first words of the writs sent out, 'Quo warranto' - by what warrant? In answer John is reputed to have drawn an old sword claiming that:-

'My ancestors coming into this land with William (the Conqueror) did obtain their lands by the sword, and I am resolved with the sword to defend them.'

John kept his tenancies, including Grantham and Stamford.

Alice had died in 1256, but John survived until 1303 and so would have been Lord of Grantham when the Cortège arrived. It is unlikely he spent much time there. He was buried, as most of his family were, in the Abbey of his chief seat of Lewes.

His only son, William, had been killed in a tournament in 1286, and, as soon as John died, the Abbot of Peterborough (St. Peter's Burgh) requested Grantham and Stamford beyond (North of) the Bridge, which, by then, the Warenne family also held. However, John was succeeded by his grandson, the posthumous John, who had married Joan of Bar, Edward and Eleanor's grand-daughter, in 1306, when he was under age (21). The marriage was not a success. It was annulled on the grounds that John had already been betrothed to Maud of Nereford when he married Joan. An engagement was then considered binding. Joan went 'beyond the sea'. John agreed to pay her 740 marks a year.

He seems to have come to an arrangement with the successive kings, Edward II and Edward III. In 1315 he made over all his property, including Grantham and Stamford, to Edward II. A proviso emerged in his agreement with Edward III, that his two sons by Maud of Nereford should be allowed to inherit certain of the properties and bear the name Warenne. John died, the last Earl of Warenne, in 1347 aged 61, when Grantham and Stamford passed to other tenants.

The ownership, however, remained with the Crown throughout. Grantham and Stamford were granted to Edward by King Henry in 1253/4 and almost immediately passed to Eleanor, who became the fourth Queen to hold them in dower. They remained in her possession until her death in 1290. The posthumous John's grandfather John, who died in 1303, must have been Eleanor's only tenant.

Grantham in 1290

Manthorpe Road enters North-east Grantham where the old town may be found.

The Castle

A mound on the north side of Grantham House, a curve in the River and a surviving 13th. century door in the street wall (*see fig. 1*) all indicate the site of the castle. The Mow Beck, flowing into the River at this point (now culverted under Brook Street and Manthorpe Road) could, with the River, have formed a wet moat.

Pevsner/Harris claim the present Grantham House has a 1380 core, which would suggest a house here replaced the castle as the Lord's dwelling about this date and it was then that the castle began to decay.

St. Wulfram's Church

Opposite the castle site stands the church, dedicated to St. Wulfram. Wulfram, Archbishop of Sens (France) trained at Fontanelle Abbey and worked as a Christian missionary in Frisia between 700 and 720. Under a new king, Radbod, the Frisians turned against Christianity, which gave the King of the Franks an excuse to attack. The defeated Radbod agreed to be baptised by Wulfram, changing his mind on being told his ancestors would be excluded from a Christian after-life.

1. The Castle Door

Wulfram returned to Fontanelle, where he died on March 20th. 720. As a saint he is usually depicted in the act of baptising King Radbod. His association with England is remote and churches dedicated to him here are rare. Apart from the church at Grantham there was one other ancient dedication - at Ovingdean near Brighton, Sussex. The St. Wulfram cult may have been brought to Grantham by

Frisians, who are believed to have joined their Saxon neighbours in invading England. By 886 Frisia and half of England, including Grantham, was in Danish hands so the connection could have come through Danish Christians.

The present building may incorporate part of the Domesday church. A stretch of Saxon style herringbone masonry, in the wall near the organ, 'tells of the 11th. century' (Pevsner/Harris), and the misalignment of the chancel and nave roofs implies the nave was a 12th. century Norman addition. Six piers of this Norman nave have survived.

On the 8th. of February 1222 the church was struck by lightning which 'put it into flames' (Matthew Paris). This destruction, together with the increasing wealth of the local wool merchants, probably activated and sustained the rebuilding and extension of the church which took place from the 13th. to the 15th. century. North and South aisles, each nearly as wide as the nave itself absorbed the transepts of the Norman building. A 13th. century doorway, mutilated for the later addition of the porch, has survived in the North aisle wall. Pevsner/Harris date the south aisle doorway c.1230, but consider it was re-sited and that the building of the South aisle continued into the 14th. century, when the upper stories of the tower were also commenced.

The Angel

There are no visible remains of the Templars' property, but it is believed the present 'Angel and Royal Hotel' stands on or near the inn's site. The oldest part of the present structure is the gateway (c.1350). It is claimed the two stone head hood mould terminals represent King Edward III (Edward and Eleanor's grandson) and Philippa of Hainault, whom he married in 1328/9. (*see fig. 2*).

King John is reputed to have stayed at the earlier hostelry and Richard III, Charles I, as well as Edward III and Queen Philippa at the present hotel. 'Royal' was added to commemorate a visit by the Prince of Wales, later King Edward VII, in 1866.

The Market Place and Cross

The Market Place was probably more extensive in 1290, covering the area now occupied by Conduit Lane (the name, at least, dating from after the Grey Friars built their conduit) Union Street (associated with workhouses) and Guildhall (named in the 19th. century). Rows are associated with markets, being the lines in which stalls selling the same produce were organised. It is possible the streets known today as Wong, and Greenwood Rows in spite of their unsuitable names which may be later fabrications, together with the more usual Butchers' Row, indicate the extent of the old market as later these rows of stalls were often replaced by more permanent structures. 'Greyfriars' is likely to recall the lane leading to the Friary, which bounded the Market Place on the South-west.

A market cross, the base consisting of four tiers of worn stone steps, octagonal in shape, surmounted by a cone and a pillar, stands in the present Market Place. It is dated from 1280, since when it has been removed and replaced at least twice (1779 and 1884 when it was stored until 1910) (*see fig.3*).

2. The 'Angel' Gate

The Franciscan Friary

According to Dugdale (Monasticum VI 1513) the Grey Friars were established in Grantham in 1290 when they were granted an Indulgence by Pope Nicholas IV (1288-1292). The daily pittances of 6s.4d and 7s. provided by Edward in 1300 suggest there were then 19 and 21 friars at 4d. each. In 1314 they were authorised to bring water to their house in leaden pipes.

At its surrender in 1541 the property consisted of a church, a belfry, the aquaduct, a garden of one acre and a number of other gardens, a small, enclosed field, called Paradise and another five acres, a Kilnhouse, stables and tenements. (V.C.H.) After being leased to Robert Bocher and David Vincent, a Court page, the Friary was sold and demolished.

The Grey Friars are remembered by the Conduit, which stands in the Market Place. This was erected in 1597 to encase and dispense water from the Friars' supply. It was probably, like that at Lincoln, initially constructed of stone from the Friary buildings, which were dismantled about that date.

Overnight Stay

On the night of December 4th. accommodation for the Court could have been provided by the Castle, the Franciscan Friary and the Templars' inn. Although the Castle was part of Eleanor's estate, and the rent paid by John Warenne for the Manor and soke had doubtless gone towards her household expenses, it did not appear to attract direct royal interest. No mention of repairs or extensions emerges in the rolls for Henry III's reign, such as are recorded for Clipstone, Lincoln and other residences at stopping places along the route. It is unlikely John Warenne himself lived in the Castle, which was administered by a bailiff, though, if he followed Bishop Grosseteste's 'Rules' he would have visited the Manor annually to inspect the accounts and estate management.

Minor Court officials may have stayed at the Castle and the Friary may have been in a position to provide some accommodation, but it is most likely Edward with his top Court administrators imitated his Grandfather, King John, and stayed at the Templars' inn.

As St. Wulfram's was the only church, there is little doubt that it was here Eleanor was laid before the High Altar and the customary vigil kept, in which the Franciscans may have joined. Although re-building must have been in progress, the chancel and nave were not included and the N. aisle was almost certainly completed. Even if the South aisle were in the process of being re-built, it is unlikely the South nave wall would have been breached before the aisle was finished, so that the nave would remain enclosed and the Church viable. The church and inn lay and lie in convenient proximity.

3. The Market Cross

Exeunt

On the morning of December 5th. the Cortège left Grantham for Stamford. For maximum publicity it would have processed down the main street to where the Chapel of St. Peter stood at the top of St. Peter's Hill. This chapel was the property of Peterborough Abbey. It was probably still on the same site as that presented to that convent, before Domesday, by the 'nun Alswith'. It is generally believed nearby was the site selected for the second of Eleanor's memorial crosses.

The Grantham Cross

This cross is not recorded in the accounts of Queen Eleanor's executors, nor is any part of it now known to exist. It was listed by Stowe (Survey) and Stukely is reputed to have seen it in situ. Michael Honeybone in 'The Book of Grantham' writes:-

'Stukeley lived on St. Peter's Hill, on the East side and, in a letter to the Earl of Oxford, he gave a brief account of the Queen Eleanor crosses, one at Grantham before his door in a large area: he has one of the lions (i.e. from the arms of either Leon or England) in his garden'.

This letter is not referred to by Piggott ('William Stukeley') indexed at the Lincolnshire Archives Office or included in the Surtees edition of 'Stukeley's Diaries and Letters'.

The most substantial evidence for the existence of this cross comes from the Grantham Corporation Minute Book for 1633-1704, which is preserved at Grantham Council House, recorded on micro-film, and being prepared for publication in book form by Bill Couth, to whom I am indebted for the following extract. The spelling has been modernised.

The Tenth Court of Richard Coney 19th. February 1646/7

At this Court, the stones which came from the Cross at the upper end of the High Street, anciently called Queen's Cross, and the Cross in Swinegate, commonly called Apple Cross, being thrown down by soldiers in the late time of war, taken into consideration, and this consideration and this Court being informed that many of the said stones are (have been) taken away, it is now ordered that the constables of every ward shall make diligent inquiry and search to find out in whose custody any of the said stones are remaining, and who has taken any of them and converted them to their own use, and to certify (inform) this Court thereof to the end the Town may receive satisfaction of the offenders for those that are taken away: and, for the remainder of the stones of both crosses, the constables are to see them to be removed to the Church (i.e. St. Wulfram's) for the use of the Corporation.

In 1652 one of the inhabitants of Grantham was prosecuted for his part in the destruction of the Cross and for using the stones to repair a wall. (Bill Couth).

Provided the Court's instructions were carried out and the stones of both crosses taken to the Church, it is unlikely those from the 'Apple Cross' and those from the Eleanor Cross were separated and identified. Should the Apple Cross be the present Market Cross, it is not impossible that its substantial steps, which have caused people in the past to confuse it with the Eleanor Cross, could, indeed be a surviving fragment.

The Civil War

Grantham was involved in the struggle between King Charles I and Parliament. The Town was taken for the King by Colonel Cavendish in 1642. On May 13th. the following year there was a battle outside the Town, in which Cromwell fought. During 1645, when Grantham was garrisoned by Parliamentarian troops under Colonel Rossiter, St. Peter's Chapel was destroyed and the Queen's Cross 'thrown down'. The townspeople, not wishing to see good stones wasted, 'converted them to their own use' which led to this action taken by the Alderman's Court the following year.

PART IV

Stamford

Grantham to Stamford

According to Leland this road was 'All in Keston (the area is still known as Kesteven) meetly good. Plenty of wood. 18 miles.' By to-day's roads it is 22 miles. The route runs parallel to the River Witham along the B1174 to Little Ponton, a Domesday manor. Here it becomes the A1. Passing through Great Ponton it comes to Colsterworth where it is joined by Ermine Street (B6403) and runs by way of South Witham. All these three are Domesday manors. At Great Casterton Edward signed a writ on December 5th. Here the Old Medieval Great North Road diverges from the present A1 which by-passes the Town. As the present B1081, the old way entered the walled town by what was St. Clement's Gate. Available evidence suggests it was outside this gate the third Eleanor Cross was erected, so that here the cross site was selected not on leaving, but on entering the Town.

The Eleanor Cross

The Site of the Cross

Stamford cross has not survived but two descriptions are given of it in situ. Captain Richard Symonds, a royalist visiting Stamford on his way from Newark to Huntingdon (B1081) in 1645 placed the cross 'in the hill before you come into the Town'. Richard Butcher, Town Clerk, in a survey of Stamford taken in 1646, stated it was near to the York highway (B1081) and about 240 (unit omitted) from Clement Gate.

In a diary entry for December 21st. 1745 and in a letter to Samuel Gale, a fellow antiquarian, dated January 6th.1746 William Stukeley records the discovery of the cross's remains. These were found on a grassy heath called by the towns-people 'Queen's Cross' (not identified): at the tumulus 'hanging on the apex or tip of high ground: and 'at the cliff about ½ mile from Stamford on the left-hand side of the road leading from Stamford to Brig (Great) Casterton' (B1081). It is possible the 'tumulus' was the one drawn by Stukeley in October 1744 and labelled 'near ½ mile in the London Road

North of Scotgate' (B1081). Stukeley also wrote to The Mercury placing the cross on the first grassy cliff on the left along the road from Stamford to Brig Casterton (B1081).

All this information can be interpreted to give approximately the same position. Butcher's missing unit is most likely to have been paces, a unit used by Speed. 240 paces or yards from the town gate along the B1081 would give a position about the junction with the A606 (Empringham Road). If Stukeley did not measure his 'about ½ mile' and 'near ½ mile' from the Town gate, known at different times as Scot Gate and St. Clement's, but from the East end of Scotgate the road, i.e. from his own church, the distance to the point given by Butcher is 3/8 mile (near ½). These measurements could all indicate the same position on the Medieval Great North Road (B1081), at its junction with the A606. On the A606 side of this junction the ground still rises so that, had the Cross been built here, on an excavated, level area, it would have been 'in the hill'.

The Appearance of the Cross

The 17th. century sitings and 18th. century excavation inform of the crosses appearance. When the tumulus was opened by Mr. Wyng, the Surveyor of the Turnpike Road, the workmen uncovered a complete lower and part of a higher tier of steps. Stukeley recorded the sides of the hexagonal - octagonal on second viewing - base as 13 foot long and the steps made of 'squared Barnack stone'. Other 'carved stones of the Barnack quarry' were in the tumulus - one a 'pyramidal' piece, belonging to 'the pinnacle work at the top adorned with roses' (A rose was Edward I's symbol).

The 'Barnack stone' compares with Butcher's 'free (easily worked) stone'. Both Butcher and Symonds refer to shields on the cross, the latter describing the arms of England, Ponthieu and Castile quartered Leon, 'often carved' (repeated).

The Fate of the Cross

The Cross was in need of repair in 1621, when Stamford Town Records for November the 30th. note that the fate of the King's Cross 'shall be forthwith amended by a sufficient workman'. Perhaps a sufficiently skilled workman could not be found, or the restoration was inadequate, for, though Captain Symonds had been able to identify Eleanor's arms in 1645, the following year, Butcher could only discern those of Castile and Leon, the others 'envious time' having 'so defaced, that only the ruins appear'.

Stukeley and his friend, Peck, Rector and Prebend of Lincoln, both believed the Cross had been destroyed by 'fanatics in the beginning of the Rebellion' (Civil War). However it appears to have survived until 1646 and there is no firm evidence that it was destroyed by Puritan inconoclasts. It had probably disappeared by 1730 when Stukeley first came to live in Stamford. Already decaying in 1646, the moveable stone was likely to have been carried away for other uses and the less portable steps, by some means, buried.

The 'stone adorned with roses' Stukeley took to his garden in Barn Hill, intending it for his 'Hermitage'. He must have taken other remnants as well, because, on leaving Stamford in 1748 he added a note to his diary stating this stone with 'many other fragments of Queen's Cross' was left in his garden when Mr. Noel bought the house. These stones have all disappeared. Stukeley's drawing of his 'Hermitage' - a grotto like structure made of antique stones - was made in 1738, before his discovery of the Cross remains.

[Based on material from The Stamford Historian (No.4) Stukeley's Diaries and Letters (Surtees Society) 3 volumes. 'William Stukeley' by Stuart Piggott.]

Stamford in 1290

Stamford, like Lincoln, had been one of the five Danish boroughs captured by Edmund, Lord of the English, in 942 (Anglo-Saxon Chronicle). It had developed as two settlements, one each side of the River Welland.

The King's Borough

The settlement North of the River was in 1290 as it had been in Domesday, the King's borough. The 'vill and castle' remained in royal hands. It had been granted to Eleanor as part of her dower on her marriage to Edward. As at Grantham, her tenants in chief were the Warennes.

The Castle

The Northern settlement was well fortified. A castle lay in the South-west corner, by the River (*'5' on Speed's map fig. 1*). Domesday, five residences had been abandoned for its building and, at an inquest held in 1341 the site was said to have covered two acres. It may have replaced an earlier castle referred to in the Anglo-Saxon Chronicle in 928.

In 1215 William of Warenne had been given the manor of Uffington for 'the upkeep of his castle at Stamford'. It was probably in use in 1290, but, by 1341, it was in a poor condition. The inquest reported the walls 'in pieces and decayed'. There was then a hall, a chapel, a prison and an 'old tower'. During the reign of Richard III (1483-1485) materials from the Castle ruins were granted to the Carmelites to repair their buildings. Finally, in 1935, the mound was levelled and the base of the tower removed to provide a car park (Pevsner/Harris).

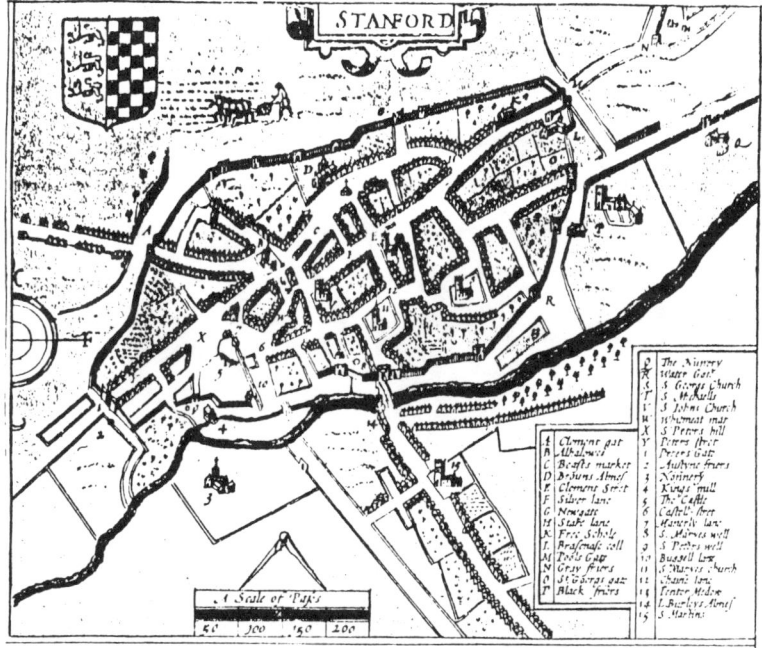

1. Speed's Map

Two remnants likely to have been part of the Castle are to be found on the North side of Bath Row. The first is a section of wall with a door and two blank indentations, well above the present ground level, on the West side of Castle Dyke at its Junction with Bath Row. (*see fig. 2*). The second, also a wall section with indentations lies between numbers 13 and 15 Bath Row.

The Castle is recalled in Castle Street and Castle Dyke.

Walls and Gates

Stamford was a walled town when beseiged by Duke Henry, later King Henry II, in 1153. Walls are shown on Speed's map, though these may follow a different line in the North-east, from those of 1290.

Of the seven main gates shown by Speed, six, St. Peter's, Clement's, Pool's (Paul's), St. George's, Watergate and Bridgegate, were likely to have been extant in 1290. Newgate on the North wall, was probably a later addition.

2. The Castle Ruins

The old walls may be followed in a clockwise direction from St. Mary's Hill through St. Mary's Passage along Bath Row, noting the Castle remains, and King's Mill. St. Peter's Vale, a steep, cobbled way, joins St. Peter's Street, where, by Hopkin's Hospital, the jambs of St. Peter's Gate may be seen. This gate was mentioned in 1341/2 when the Austin Friars moved nearby.

In the first street on the right a substantial bastion of the old town wall has survived (*see fig. 3*). Turning right again, West Street crosses Scotgate, the main road to the North which was barred by St. Clement's Gate marked by a pier dated 1780 (Pevsner/Harris).

The Postern in Barn Hill

In the garden wall of 9, Barn Hill (Stukeley House) a postern may be seen. It consists of a central doorway and an aperture on either side, one with steps leading downwards. Stukeley, having reputedly witnessed the victorious but mutilated English, returning, on foot in pouring rain from the Battle of Culloden Moor (near Inverness) in 1746 had an inscription, not popular with Scottish visitors, carved above this gate. By then it was part of his Barn Hill garden, and not in its original position. This is believed to have been the postern by which King Charles I left Stamford when passing through on his way to Scotland at the end of April 1646. (*see fig. 4*).

After Scotgate, West Street becomes North Street and then East Street. There is nothing of the old North wall to be seen on this stretch. The square corner made by East Street and Brazenose Lane, suggests an alteration to the line of the earlier wall, possibly to accommodate Brazenose College which was established here after 1290.

3. Wall Bastion

St. Paul's Gate (Pool's on Speed's map) barred St. Paul's Street, which gave access to the Franciscan Friary. Brazenose Lane continues to meet St. Leonard's Street, which led to St. Leonard's Priory. The gate on this Street, Speed's St. George's, was removed in 1806. A plaque commemorating this gate may be seen on the wall of the 'Daniel Lambert', a hostelry celebrating Stamford's heaviest man.

Wharf Road equates happily with the line of the medieval wall. About half way along was a gate (Speed's Watergate) which allowed passage to and from the Tenter

Field, remembered in Tenter Court, where the cloth was stretched to dry on tenter frames and hooks. Wharf Road continues to Bridge Gate and so completes the circuit of the Town walls.

4. Stukeley's Gate and Garden

The Cloth Trade

A reference in the Anglo-Saxon Chronicle suggests there was a market in Stamford in 963. By the 13th. century the Town's trade was largely concerned with clothing and cloth. In the Liberate rolls of King Henry III several Stamford merchants are named and Court purchases of robes, cloth and furs are recorded. It appears to have been the custom to provide new liveries at Court 'against Witsuntide'. One order (1249) consisted of 6 cloths of scarlet, 12 of burnet (a fine dark brown woollen cloth) and 12 of Stamford Blue (Lincoln was famous for its green). King Henry also bought robes for Edward (1243).

Like Lincoln, Stamford had a Jewish community. They were persecuted 1189/90; investigated 1268/9, when their chests of documents were seized and taken to London; and driven out in the general expulsion of 1290.

Jousting

After jousting became organized and controlled, one of the Country's licensed tilting grounds lay on the Medieval Great North Road, South of Stamford. Jousts gave the Earls and their followers an opportunity to muster. This was probably why, on two occasions during the 13th. century, in 1215, prior to Magna Carta and in 1225, when the Earls supported Henry III's younger brother, Richard, against the King, they had met at Stamford.

The Wars of the Roses

Much of Stamford was destroyed during the Lancastrian attack of 1461. The subsequent rebuilding and use of salvaged material have created problems in the architectural dating of surviving buildings.

Stamford Churches in 1290

At Domesday, Stamford was entered under Lincolnshire, Rutland and Northamptonshire. Four churches are recorded. St. Peter's, belonging to Albert the Clerk (of Lorraine) is mentioned under all three counties. A church held by Falstolf from the King, and two churches 'in these wards' which Earnwine, the priest, had held prior to 1087, are under Lincolnshire. In the notes (to the Phillimore edition) it is suggested Earnwine's two churches were St. Clement's in Scotgate and All Saints by the Water. St. Peter's, St. Clement's and two churches dedicated to All Saints are recorded in the 13th. century Court rolls.

There was a reference to St. Peter's Stamford in 1254 and, in 1292 a St. Peter's 'near Stamford' was granted to

Sempringham. It is not marked on Speed's map, but the site has been preserved as a green area in St. Peter's Street, near St. Peter's Gate.

St. Clement's, Scotgate, which has also disappeared, had been conferred on the nuns of the Priory of St. Michael, which lay South of the River (3 on Speed's map 'nonnery') in the reign of King John. It was incorporated into the parish of St. John the Baptist which had been founded c.1450 (V on Speed's map) during the 16th. century. The bar across Scotgate is Clement Gate on Speed's map and was still so called during the 18th. century.

An All Saint's was also held by the Nuns of St. Michael and confirmed as their property in 1227. In 1434 it was amalgamated with another of the Nuns' churches, St. Martin's in the Southern Settlement (15 on Speed's map) and subsequently disappeared. It was not immediately forgotten. In the Reign of Henry VIII (1509-1546) there is a reference to the 'parish of St. Martin's, late All Hallows' (i.e. All Saints').

At the time of the amalgamation this church was placed 'beyond the Bridge' suggesting it was across the River from St. Martin's, in the King's Burgh, but sufficiently near to allow the joining of the parishes i.e. 'by the water' so this Church could have been the Domesday "All Saints by the Water'.

A church dedicated to All Saints stands 'at the hub' of Stamford today. Architectural evidence dates it from at least the 13th. century. It was substantially renovated by the merchants William and John Browne in the 15th. century. Stukeley, the antiquarian, was vicar here from 1730 to 1747.

Another early church to have survived is St. Paul's. It was used as a schoolroom for Radcliff's Grammar School (Free School K on Speed's map). It is now incorporated into Stamford School Chapel and may be seen from St. Paul's Street.

In the mid 12th. century two Stamford churches, dedicated to St. Mary, were held by Durham (Dugdale 'Monasticum'). The more important has not survived, though, as it was mentioned in connection with St. Mary's Gild in 1392 (Patent), it would have been extant in 1290.

It stood 'at the Bridge'. St. Mary's Well (8 on Speed's map) denotes the site. The Norman archway giving access from St. Mary's Hill to St. Mary's Passage probably belonged to this Church.

The other Durham church, St. Mary the Less (Bennewerk) still stands at the top of St. Mary's Hill. There is a small 13th. century window in the S. vestry (Pevsner/Harris) and the West doorway has Norman components. It is '11' on Speed's map.

St. George's, 'S' on Speed, may be found in St. George's Square. It is an architectural mixture, having possibly suffered fire damage in the 13th. century and being partly rebuilt in the 14th. In the next century William Bruges, then Garter King of Arms added the chancel and clerestory. It was further enlarged and made cruciform in 1888. In 1290 there was likely to have been a much smaller St. George's probably in a ruined state.

The parish of Holy Trinity was mentioned in a land grant made to the Carmelites in 1285 and a Patent roll of 1392. The church stood on the corner of St. Paul's Street opposite Brazenose Lane outside the Town walls. The site is marked by a plaque. It does not appear on Speed's map and was probably one of the churches destroyed in 1461.

The church of St. Andrew was also extant in 1290 and probably destroyed in 1461. Its site is unknown.

The Friaries of Stamford in 1290

The Friars of the Sack

Of the four friaries extant in 1290 only one lay on the West side of the Town; The Friary of the Penance of Jesus Christ. It was, of course, subject to the general closure and the Friary was replaced by that of the Austin Friars c. 1341.

The Austin Friary, and so that of the Sack Friars, was placed by Leland in the western suburb hard by St. Peter's Gate, which corresponds with the position (2) given by Speed.

The three other friaries all lay outside the Town on the East.

The Franciscan Friary

Speed shows the Gray Friars at 'N' c.125 paces along the road from 'Pool's' (St. Paul's) Gate, that is St. Paul's Street. The Friary lies in the fork between two roads (Ryall Road - the A6121 and Uffingham Road - the A16) placing it on the site of the present hospital. Speed shows the great gatehouse, which still stands, and the boundary walls remnants of which Peck saw in the 18th. century. During the 19th. century this gateway came to be identified with the Carmelites, but now it is accepted as part of the Franciscan Friary. Dugdale described it as bearing 'three coats of arms, central England and France and others defaced and three niches for statues'. On the rear are the arms of Henry Foyer, who financed the building of the Hospital in 1828. (*see fig. 5*).

91

5. The Franciscan Friary Gate - Arms of Henry Foyer

The Franciscans were established in Stamford before 1229/30, when they were granted wood for fuel. In 1235 they received wood for the stalls of their church. (V.C.H.)

Joan of Kent, mother of King Richard II by her second husband the 'Black Prince', was buried at the Grey Friars in 1385. In June 1386 Richard ordered the immediate repair of the glass in the chapel. (Patent)

At the Dissolution the Friary was demanded by Charles Brandon, brother-in-law to Henry VIII, and was granted by him in 1541. The site then covered 11 acres but the main buildings had been destroyed.

The Carmelite Friary

The White Friars were established in Stamford by 1268, when they were building their church, dedicated to the Virgin Mary. (Monasticum). It has been suggested (V.C.H.) their founder was Henry de Hanna, Provincial of the Carmelites from 1254-1271, who was buried in the Church.

This Friary, being the furthest north-east, is off Speed's map. It was situated 'just at the eastern end of the Franciscan Friary'. At the Dissolution it had been suggested that the two sites could have been amalgamated to provide a single palace for the King. It was, however, granted to Richard Cecil, whose son, William is credited with having entertained Queen Elizabeth there, while Burley House was being built (1574-1787).

The Dominican Friary

The Black Friars (P on Speed's map) were established outside the Town wall, between St. George's Gate and Water Gate, before 1241 when they were granted 2s. In 1243/4 they were building a refectory and installing a water system. Their church was in use by 1260 and rebuilt in 1310 (V.C.H.)

Leland confirms Speed's siting, adding 'their convent took up a large parcel of ground. There is a house built on the ruins of it and belongs to Savil Cust, Esq.'

St. Leonard's Priory

There is a case for St. Leonard's Priory having been founded by St. Wilfrid (634-709). Bede stated Egfrith gave him 10 hides of land at Stanforda. In the 15th. century the Prior, John Wessington, identified 'Stanforda' with Stamford, Lincs. Though King of Northumbria, Egfrith had conquered Lindsay in 674 so this land would, then, have been in his gift. Wilfrid was with the Christian community on Lindisfarne, which transferred to Durham. St. Leonard's was a cell of Durham.

St. Leonard is the patron saint of prisoners. He was a popular saint in the Middle Ages with 177 early dedications. It was customary for released prisoners to hang their chains in his churches.

Remains of what was probably the Priory Church may be seen in a field at the East end of Priory Road, well outside the medieval town walls, 'Q' The Nunnery, on Speed's map. Norman pillars with leaf and geometric carving preserved on their inner sides, belong to an early phase (12th. century) of building. The West front was a later addition but pre-dates 1290. The wall behind the pillars is more recent. (*see fig. 6*)

On November 2nd. a new Prior, Geoffrey of Boston, was presented. He resigned on January 8th. 1292, so was likely to have been Prior when Eleanor's Cortège visited Stamford. Although the Priory did not lie on the route which the Court was most likely to have followed, it merits a visit from anyone interested in the period.

The Academic Tradition; Stamford and Oxford

A studium had been established at Oxford by 1133. Until 1274 students had been divided into 'nations' i.e. Northerners (North of the Trent) and Southerners (South of the Trent). Disagreements arose, both between the 'nations' and between students and the townspeople ('town and gown'). In 1209, 1238, 1261 and 1334 the violence generated by these disagreements led to student migrations.

In 1209, Oxford lost students to Cambridge and in

subsequent migrations, royal intervention was sought and students were ordered to return to Oxford. It is claimed, after the 1261 migration to Northampton, though some students complied, others settled in Stamford.

The famous exodus was that of the Brazenose students in 1334. It was their arrival in Stamford which resulted in the establishment of Brazenose College, remembered in Brazenose Lane, which probably altered the course of the town wall and the position of St. Paul's Gate. Oxford's reaction to this exodus, the exaction of an oath not to teach in Stamford from all their graduates, suggests Stamford was regarded as a serious academic threat.

6. St. Leonard's Priory

Stamford as a Seat of Learning

Stamford's early academic tradition was connected with St. Leonard's Priory and the Carmelite Friary under Henry de Hanna. Leland wrote:-

'Sometime readings of Liberal Sciences were at Stamford. The names of Peterborough Hall, Sempringham and Vauldier yet remain as places for those houses of men of religion that send their scholars there to study.'

He is referring to Sempringham Hall, St. Peter's Street, founded and endowed by Robert Lutteral, Rector of Irnham in 1292 and given to the Priory of Sempringham and the educational establishments of the Abbey of Val Dieu, Grimsthorpe Park, and Peterborough. Eleanor left a legacy of 200 marks to the Master of Oxford University.

The Cortège in Stamford

The signing of the writ at Great Casterton together with the siting of the Cross outside St. Clement's Gate confirm that the Cortège entered by Scotgate. The night could have been spent at any of the Friaries or / and at the Castle. If the King had stopped at the Castle, Eleanor's body could have lain in the chapel there. Of the Friaries that of the Dominicans was the most likely choice. It lay close to the Town, Chapters held there in 1247, 1261 and 1276 suggest it was able to accommodate large numbers. The Black Friars were particularly associated with the royal family and Edward II did stay at the Dominican Friary, Stamford in 1309 and Edward III in 1332 and 1335 (V.C.H.)

The Grey and White Friaries, and, of course, St. Leonard's Priory, were less conveniently situated and the White Friars the least well established of the religious houses. The Sack Friary, though more convenient, was probably much reduced in 1290, having but four inmates in 1300 (V.C.H.)

An overnight stay at the Castle and the Black Friary, just outside Water Gate, would offer the Cortège quick and easy access to the Bridge Gate for an early start on its 19 mile journey to the Royal Palace at Geddington.

St. Mary's Hill

At some time during their transit through Stamford it would have been necessary for the Cortège to have passed down St. Mary's Hill, which connected the Bridge with the Medieval town centre.

On the West side, number 11 incorporates what is often referred to as 'Packhorse Arch'. According to Pevsner/Harris this is part of a Norman house. By the side of number 13, opposite the Town Hall, is a vault dated c.1220 which may also have been part of the house.

Stamford Baron

The settlement on the South bank of the River was held by the Abbot and Convent of St. Peter's Burgh. It was on land 'stretching from the Welland to the River Nene' allegedly given to the first Abbot, Saxwulf, by Wulfere of Mercia in 656. At Domesday, the tribute and toll of 'the ward across the bridge' were recognised as the Abbot's. Because it was held by the Abbot (technically a baron) and not the King, the southern settlement became known as Stamford Baron.

Later, the Abbey of (Peter) Burgh lost Stamford Baron to 'a certain knight' (Chronicles of Hugh Candidas) but it was recovered from his heir by Abbot William Waterville (deposed 1175). This Abbot also acquired 14 messuages for the Abbey, in the Northern settlement. The Abbey had held 10 properties there at Domesday. It is likely an early bridge across the Welland had been built by the Peterborough monks to facilitate the administration of these properties North of the River. (*Fig. 7 - The River Welland*).

The Cortège in Stamford Baron

In order to reach Geddington it was necessary to cross the River Welland. The simplest way to do this was by the Bridge Gate and main bridge, which stood as it does today. West from the bridge the River is shown on Speed's map, and may still be seen, to divide into two. The more northerly served the King's mill, valued at Domesday Record at 30s. It is '4' on Speed's map. The present King's Mill dates from c.1700 and is now used as a Play School centre. The more southerly flow worked the Abbot of Peterborough's mill, now disappeared. At Domesday, it was valued at 40s.

The Hospital of St. John the Baptist and St. Thomas the Martyr

The Cortège route lay past the Hospital, situated 'at the South end of Stamford Bridge' (Leland). It was on the West side. Lord Burley's Almshouses now stand on the site.

This Hospital had been established for the relief of all poor. The founders were named in a confirmation charter of 1290 as Siward, who gave a house and chapel; Brand de Fossato, said to have been a wealthy monk of Peterborough Abbey, who gave land and possessions; Richard Humet and Bertram Verdun, who gave a meadow at the South end of the Bridge. Humets were Lords of Stamford before the Warennes. The line had failed by 1256 so the Hospital must have been founded before that date, and probably during the reign of Richard I (1189-1199).

Lord Burley's almshouses were built after the Dissolution. Pevsner claims they are raised on Norman foundations and, at the East corner of the river frontage a Norman arch and flat buttress may be seen. The Almshouses are 14 on Speed's map.

7. The River Welland - dividing for the King's Mill and the Abbot's Mill

The Nunnery of St. Michael

On the west side of the main street which ran through Stamford Baron, lay a large nunnery '3' on Speed's map. Hugh Candidus described how William de Waterville, Abbot of Peterborough, established this house of 40 nuns, dedicated to St. Michael, and gave the nuns the Church of St. Martin's - now on the opposite side of the main street.

Subsequent Abbots granted the nuns the churches of St. Clement, All Saints and St. Andrew, as well as other gifts. In 1291 the Nunnery was valued at £66.13s.4d (Pope Nicholas Tax). In 1299 the buildings included a chamber, a hall, cellar, kitchen and bakehouse. By the 18th. century Peck claimed 'Nothing of the monastery was standing but the site was known as the Nuns in St. Martin's' (i.e. Parish).

St. Martin's

The earlier church was probably destroyed in the Lancastrian attack of 1461. The present Church of St. Martin's dates from c.1481. It houses the tomb of William Cecil, Lord Burghley, Queen Elizabeth I's Lord High Treasurer and principal minister. The stained glass was removed from this Church by a Mr. Popple 'so that he should not have to use his spectacles' (Stukeley).

Holy Sepulchre and St. Giles

This small house was situated on the South side of the present George Hotel. It is claimed that parts have survived in the house adjoining the Hotel.

The Hospital of St. Giles, lay outside Stamford Baron and was probably for Lepers. There were orders for repairs in the 14th. century and it seems to have disappeared after 1332.

The road to Geddington (A43) turned off westwards before St. Giles, leaving the Medieval Great North Road to rejoin Ermine Street and continue on its way towards London.

A Change of Route

The most direct way from Stamford to London, and that usually followed by the Court was Southwards through the Soke of Peterborough, Huntingdon, Braughing, Ware and Waltham. For some reason the Cortège crossed from the Ermine Street route to Watling Street, by way of Geddington and Northampton, adding about 25 miles to their journey.

The reasons for such a diversion can only be surmised. It seems unlikely that Edward would feel any scruples over crossing the Abbot of Peterborough's Soke, as he had already passed through Stamford Baron. Although Edward was involved in a property dispute with the Abbot, there was nothing to suggest this was in any way acrimonious. Relations between them were sufficiently cordial for the King to ask prayers for Eleanor's soul from the Abbey and convent and provide means for them to feed 200 poor on the anniversary of the Queen's death.

The route change may have been prompted by the need to revictual. Geddington with its Chase lay on the edge of the King's forest of Rockingham. The Court had recently been at both Geddington and Northampton Castle and may have left supplies there.

An inland move to avoid flooding would also have been a possible cause. Ermine Street skirted the fens below Peterborough. In 1290 Ely was an island. Effective fen drainage did not commence until the 17th. century.

Crossing the River Nene still presented a problem in the 16th. century. Camden wrote:-

'Four or five miles from its source the Nene overflowed the plain far and near in the Winter and sometimes through the greater part of the year so that it seemed to be a vast level ocean' (Britannia).

He was probably mistaken in the source of the Nene as the flood plain would have been more distant than 4 or 5 miles away. Ermine Street did however, lie across the fuller flows of the Nene and Ouse, while Watling Street crossed these rivers nearer to their sources. The remains of the medieval stone bridge was found in the River Nene (Margery) so at some point it must have collapsed.

Edward and his followers on horseback, unencumbered by the baggage train, could have forded the waters, as a Courtier who felt he could safely defy Edward from an opposite river bank discovered to his cost (The Brut). The Clerk of the Marshalsea, responsible for transporting the Royal Household, may have considered a dryer route the more prudent choice for the Queen's Cortège.

PART V

Geddington

Stamford to Geddington

The way to Geddington lay through the Royal Forest of Rockingham. A route may be traced by way of the Domesday manors of Easton-on-the-Hill, Collyweston, Duddington, Blatherwycke, Deene, Weldon and Stanion, approximating to the present A43.

At Easton-on-the-Hill the church of All Saints with its 12th. century aisle and 13th. century vestry and South chapel, still stands. Pevsner also noted a slab, commemorating Richard de Lindon and his wife, dated 1255. The Priest's House (N.T.) is later, but incorporates a village museum.

Although the Collyweston area was inhabited by Romano-British, it has virtually no Medieval remains, having been largely re-built when in the possession of Lord Cromwell.

The Church of St. Mary at Duddington dates from at least the middle of the 12th. century. The tower was raised during the next century. Just over a mile (c.2km.) after Duddington, a road through the Domesday manors of Wakerley, Harringworth and Gretton led to Rockingham Castle.

Rockingham Castle

A pre-Conquest castle was replaced by William I. By 1249/50 William's castle was in poor condition - the keep being cracked. Maintenance and improvements had been carried out under Henry III and Edward I. In the latter's reign the chapel had been replaced and much attention given to the King and Queen's rooms. The usual attributes of a Norman castle were mentioned, towers, walls, a drawbridge, hall, solar, and a spiral staircase. Rockingham did not, however, receive one of the eight baths made at royal residences by William Aquarius (the water-carrier) in 1209/10.

The 'King's castle at Rockingham' was held, in 1290, by a constable, who was also the seneschal of the Forest. Richard of Holebroke had been appointed in 1282 and his contract has survived. He was to pay £80 p.a. rent, receive certain benefits and be responsible for repairs. For these he was entitled to take materials from the Forest.

In September 1290, Edward and Eleanor had visited Rockingham Castle (Wardrobe Accounts). Complaints had been made to the King concerning Holebroke's use of wood in the Forest. Possibly as a result of an inquiry, he was replaced as Constable by Elias of Hamul. (Hymel?).

The gatehouse and gatehouse wall date from the 13th. century. Leland, on his visit, noted the strength of the fortifications but the ruinous condition of 'the lodgings within'. This has been rectified by later Tudor, Stuart and 19th. century rebuilding.

The Court did not, this time, take the road to Rockingham, but continued along the more southerly route towards Fineshade Abbey. Bridges (History of Northamptonshire) wrote:-

'Here was originally a castle named Castle Hymel in Laxton parish, demolished in the reign of King John. Upon the ruins of it was afterwards erected a Priory of Black Canons to the honour of the Virgin Mary. It was first called the Priory of St. Mary, Castle Hymel. In later records it is named Finesheved or Fineshed Priory, which name it still (18th. century) retains'.

A confirmation printed in 'Monasticum' points to Richard Engaine, who died 1208, a forebear of the wolf slayer of Laxton, as the Founder.

At the Dissolution the 7 acre site passed to Lord Russell and then to Sir Robert Kirkham. During the 18th. century 'Mr. Kirkham' built a house on the Priory foundations. Pevsner claimed the 18th. century stables remained.

In 1290 the Prior was Thomas of Tachebrok (1288-1305).

Blatherwycke and Bulwick lay next along the route. The former was a Domesday manor. Its church, Holy Trinity, has a Norman tower. Bulwick developed later, being associated with the Fitzurse family. Reginald Fitzurse had been one of Thomas Becket's murderers. Its Church, St. Nicholas has a c.1200 arcade and a late 13th. century chancel. From Bulwick to Deene the old footpath (Jurassic Way) deviates from the A43, so that it would not have been necessary to cross Willow Brook. At Deene, the next Domesday manor, the 13th. century church of St. Peter was substantially rebuilt in the 19th. century. Deene Park, once the home of Lord Cardigan who led the 'Charge of the Light Brigade', has, according to Pevsner, a 13th. or 14th. century archway jamb in the East wing.

Weldon was entered as two manors at Domesday, Little Weldon lying first on the route. Pevsner identifies a Roman villa here, North of the A43, and dates the South arcade of the Church of St. Mary late 13th. century. Weldon stone quarries lie either side of the A43, west of the present village. The use of Weldon stone for the building of the medieval St. Paul's, London, indicates that the quarries would have been working in 1290.

Stanion, the last Domesday village before Geddington, possesses a church, St. Peter's, which Pevsner dates late 13th. century.

Geddington : The Royal Palace

At Domesday, Geddington was a small manor. The King held one hide. St. Edmund's Abbey (Bury St. Edmund) was the other landowner with one hide, one virgate: land for two ploughs, in all worth 6s. There is no mention of a church or priest under Northamptonshire although there is physical evidence for a Saxon church. It may have been administered by St. Edmund's Abbey.

A royal residence was established at Geddington prior to 1188 when Henry II's Council met there. It was probably then a hunting lodge in the Forest of Rockingham, on the River Ise.

The Liberate rolls of Henry III show how this residence changed. In 1225 Robert de Hotet was engaged for 298 days to construct petards and mangonels and, in 1244 palings were ordered to protect the hall and chapel doors. The priority then was apparently fortification, but 1244 was a pivotal year. The 1244-1254 building programme was aimed at creating a larger and more luxurious residence.

In the 'Great Hall' two windows, with columns, were to be added to the 'others' and two small round windows above these, together with the gable window, glazed. In the 'white glass' of the last, a central image of the King, presumably in coloured glass, was to be placed. Windows were to be added to the Queen's gallery and to the gable of the Countess of Leicester's chamber. The Countess was Henry III's sister, Eleanor, who had married Simon de Montfort in 1238.

The royal rooms were enlarged and improved. Queen Eleanor of Provence's wardrobe (a place to store valuables, clothes and dress) was lengthened and, in 1249 a small wardrobe with a fireplace was to be inserted between the King's audience chamber and private room. The latter was to be extended '15 or 16 feet' from the wardrobe, and the Queen's privy chamber, wardrobe and chamber were all to be widened. In 1254 the old panelling from the King's chamber was to be transferred to the Chapel and that from behind his bed replaced by green panelling decorated with small gilt shields.

As well as the King's and Queen's suites, at least one guest room the Great Hall and Chapel, the Palace had a kitchen, cellar to accommodate the 8 tuns of wine usually ordered in Henry III's time, a falcons' mews and house for the royal Falconer, which needed repairs in 1271.

The growing number of Court officials had to be housed. In 1244 a 'chamber and wardrobe for the King's Almoner' were added in the courtyard. Five years later a 'small room and other apurtenances' were built, by the Chapel, for the use of the chaplains. An extra room was constructed above the gate.

The Fate of the Palace

In 1299 Edward I granted the manor of Geddington to his son and heir, Edward. It was then valued at £48. Leland, Camden and Stukeley all recorded their visits to Geddington. By Camden's time the Palace had already disappeared although he notes 'the gatehouse was repaired in 1610 and still stands'. Stukeley placed the royal seat North-east of the Church 'in a close called Castle or Hall's Close'. He found the ground uneven and many foundations still (1742) visible. The site is now occupied by old people's homes.

The Church of St. Mary Magdalene

The pointed arcading, running along the wall, above the arches inside Geddington Church, indicate the nave was the early Saxon church, this arcading having been on its outside walls. The window cutting this arcading at the East end of the nave, 'appears to be a late Saxon insertion' (Pevsner).

Outside the Church, an early sun-dial, possibly from the Saxon building, has been incorporated in the present South aisle wall.

In the late 12th. century the Church was enlarged by the addition of a North aisle. The North wall of the Saxon church was then opened by archways, semicircular arches being supported by rounded piers with volute and waterleaf capitals (*see fig. 1*), the top section of the wall, with the Saxon arcading being left in tact.

This was the side of the Church adjacent to the palace and it was in the North wall of this aisle that the 'King's Door' was constructed to provide an easy and private way between the Church and Palace. The steps leading down from this door, into the Church were removed in 1857. It is hoped they will now be replaced and the 'King's Door' put into use. (*see fig. 1*).

1. The King's Door with Norman Pier.
(Photo by the Rev. Richard Dorrington)

The South aisle, added towards the end of the 13th. century, was either new or unfinished in 1290. The chancel and tower were constructed after 1300.

An early rood screen, claimed for both the 13th. and 14th. centuries, is now the first screen on the left in the Lady Chapel. Here may also be seen the recumbant effigy of a priest, holding a chalice and missal (13th. century. Pevsner). There are two unusual carvings in the Chancel which may pre-date the chancel itself. One of a comically unhappy kneeling figure is known as 'The King's Jester'. The other, a face with flowing hair and beard, is believed to personify the River Ise.

In 1290 the incumbent was Galf de Gropes, who had been appointed in April.

The Cross

Geddington Cross, the first one on the route to have survived, (*fig. 2*) stands outside the Church. It is more slender and delicate than other known crosses, having only three sides, instead of the more usual six or eight.

2. Geddington Cross
(Drawing by Jill Sturman)

Because it is not Gothic in style, it has been dated later than other crosses (1294 Pevsner). However, the 'stone lacework' suggests the Moorish architecture of Spain and, considering Eleanor's Castile and Aragon connections it is possible this cross was not necessarily the product of a different year, but of craftsmen from a different country. (*see fig. 3*).

3. Cross - detail of stonework with Church behind.
(Photo by the Rev. Richard Dorrington)

A Spanish Cross?

Although Geddington Cross is not overtly recorded in the accounts of Queen Eleanor's executors, there is an obscure entry under Hilary (Spring) Term 1291, which runs as follows:-

Expensae. Item. Dominico Garciae de Yspanna pro una cruce data reginae de praecepto domini J. de Berewyke. XXXs.

Omitting 'Dominico' which cannot be translated intelligibly, the remainder could read:-

To Garcia of Spain in return for one cross having been given to the Queen by order of Lord J (ohn) de Berwick (One of the Queen's chief executors) 30 shillings.

It is assumed this referred to a small cross provided for Eleanor on her death bed - 30 shillings being an appropriate amount for such a cross, but this raises the questions of why the word 'given' is then used, and why John of Berwick was involved.

'Dominico' appears to identify this Garcia, differenciating him from Garcia the Spaniard, the Keeper of the Queen's Horses and from John Garcia, a messenger from Eleanor's cousin, the Countess of Biscay, who both appear elsewhere. Garcias had been early Kings of Navarre.

It would be attractive to believe the cross at Geddington was a memorial from Eleanor's native country - a gift from her nephew Sancho, one of her cousins or from her prospective son-in-law, King Alfonso of Aragon. In the last event, however, there could have been some difficulties as Alfonso died in 1291.

Inevitably the Geddington cross has been much restored. Stukeley wrote:-

'The Duke (of Montague) has ordered the steps to be new done and the whole repaired in an elegant manner' (Diary September 6th. 1742). Bridges (History of Northamptonshire) claimed it was 'neither injured by time, like that at Waltham Cross nor altered like that near Northampton by modern additions'. A print of 1788 does show it in use as a sun-dial however.

The cross was restored by English Heritage in 1987.

The Cortège in Geddington

It was most likely the King stayed at the Royal Palace, where he had spent August 30th and 31st. and September 1st., with Eleanor earlier in the year. Eleanor's body could have reposed in the Palace Chapel, but this may have been small and inaccessible. The Church of St. Mary Magdalene would have been convenient to the Palace by the 'King's Door' and offer better facilities for public mourning and prayer.

It is possible more than one night was spent at Geddington. After Stamford the pace at which the Cortège had been travelling was reduced. An extra night was spent either at Stamford, Geddington or Northampton. The two last, offering royal residences are more likely.

PART VI

Northampton

Geddington to Northampton

To reach Northampton from the Palace and Church of Geddington it was necessary to cross the River Ise. The 13th. century bridge still stands (*see fig. 1*). To-day the route lies along the A43 which passes by or near Weekly, Kettering, Broughton, Hardwick and Sywell. Pevsner found 13th. century or pre-13th. century remnants in churches at Weekly (St. Mary's), Broughton (St. Andrew's), Hardwick (St. Leonard's), and Sywell (St. Peter and Paul), and early 14th. century work in St. Peter and Paul at Kettering. It would appear the line of the A43 is essentially the same as the road of 1290.

1. The 13th. century Bridge over the River Ise at Geddington

Sywell lies on the outskirts of Northampton. As the road enters the suburbs it passes near to Abingdon Abbey.

This is now a museum. Little of the medieval Abbey remains. The A43, or Kettering Road, enters the Town as Abingdon Street. (See 'F' on Speed's Map of Northampton *fig. 2*).

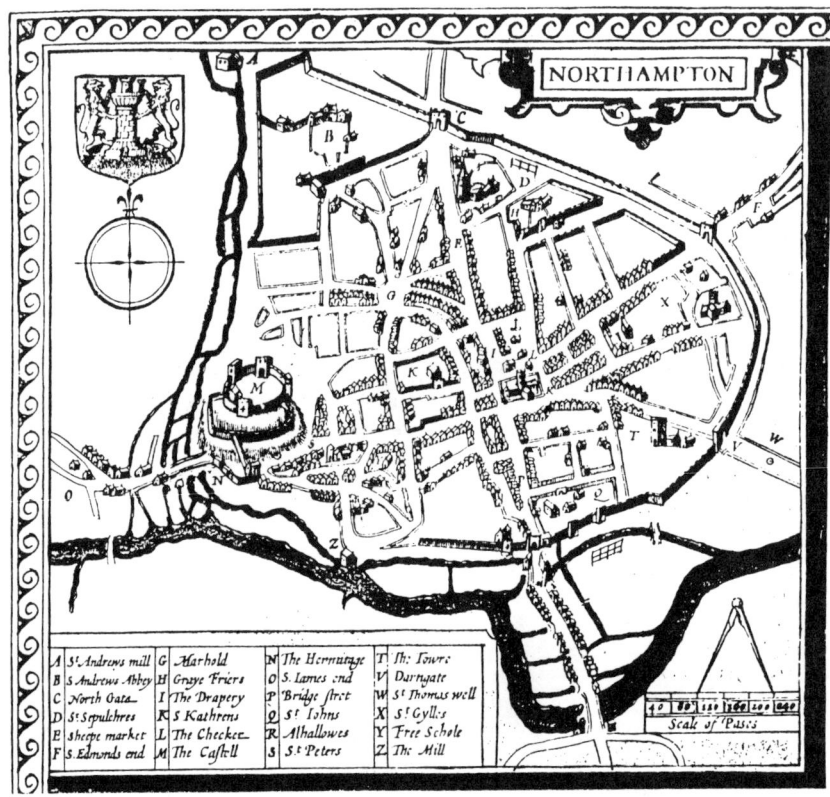

2. Speed's Map

Northampton and the Senlis Family

Medieval Northampton was predominantly a Norman settlement, shaped by the Senlis family, its first Earls. Simon of Senlis (about 25 miles North of Paris) was a protege of William the Conqueror. He married Matilda, William's great niece and the grand-daughter of Siward (the Saxon Earl of Northumberland who fought Macbeth) and was created Earl of Northampton and Huntingdon. He died returning from the Holy Land, where he had taken part in the first crusade in 1111, and was buried at the Priory of St. Mary, La Charite sur Loire, France.

David I, King of Scotland, with an eye to the vacant Earldom of Northumberland, married Simon's widow (1113) and so became step-father and guardian to her son, Simon Senlis II. This Simon, as the second Earl of Northampton, married Isabel, a daughter of Robert of Leicester, one of King Stephen's justiciars and sided with Stephen against the Empress Matilda. At the 'Joust of Lincoln' (1141) Simon was one of the five Earls whose flight led to the defeat and capture of the King. He was dead by 1153, being succeeded by Simon Senlis, the third Earl of Northampton, who died in 1184 without male issue. Both the second and third Earls were buried in Northampton at St. Andrew's Priory.

(Based on material, with some rationalization, from Dugdale's 'Baronage').

The Medieval Town Walls

Northampton was a walled town. The initial walling, ascribed to Simon Senlis I, was probably circular. In 1278 the walls were crenellated. A walkway round them, it was claimed, was used by 'burgesses of the Town, especially the sick' to take the air, and by the night-watchmen, who used the crenelles to watch for 'malefactors who might approach the Town'.

A substantial murage grant, made to the Town in 1301, implies either large scale wall repairs or extension. It has been suggested (Cox) the walls were extended and that the Tower ('T' on Speed's Map, *fig.2*) was, initially part of the earlier wall, St. Giles' Church and St. Andrew's Priory ('X' and 'B' on Speed's map) being then outside the walls.

The destruction by fire of 'three parts' (Register for Marriages All Saints' Church) of the Medieval town allowed a planned re-building. However the modern layout of the town centre bears a close resemblance to that of the medieval one. Present roads follow the line of the old walls.

Town Wall Walk

The A43 gives access to the Town through the old East Gate (near 'F' - St. Edmunds's End on Speed's map). In a clockwise direction the Medieval walls approximated to York Road and Cheyne Walk though they may have passed West of St. Giles' in 1290. Here Speed shows Dern Gate ('V') referred to in 1274/5 (Hundred Rolls). The more recent Victoria Promenade leads to the South Gate which gave access to a bridge over the River Nene and the road to London. (A508) via Watling Street. Speed shows the wall continuing to about the traffic island on St. Peter's Way, and, after a break, to approximately the Castle Bridge (A428) so it would seem that the wall here was continuous, following the line of St. Peter's Way to Black Lion Hill.

The Castle covered the South-west corner from Black Lion Hill to near Scarletwell Street, and from Chalk Lane on the East, across St. Andrew's Way to the old line of the River Nene (which was moved West to accommodate the 19th. century railway station).

The line of the wall dividing the Town from St. Andrew's Priory follows Spring Lane, Lower Harding Street and Grafton Street. The North Gate ('C' on Speed's map) stood at the junction of Grafton and Campbell Street. The latter with Upper and Lower Mounts completes the circuit to the A43 entry.

The Castle

There is no mention of a castle at Northampton in the Domesday record. Camden attributes the building of the first castle there to Simon Senlis I. It has been suggested an earthwork ('D' on fig. 3) now destroyed was the early castle. It is likely this had been a timber structure. Renn suggests it was built over late Saxon houses and notes a second phase of building 1100-1111. (Norman Castles in Britain).

Although the male line of the Senlis family did not fail until 1184 the Castle was in the King's hands before that, possibly by 1130 (Pipe Roll) and certainly in 1164 when Henry II held his council there.

Serjeantson's 'Plan of Northampton Castle' (V.C.H.) and the drawings which accompanied an article by 'T.C.R.' published in the 'Gentleman's Magazine in 1800 (*see fig.3*) show a motte and bailey castle with a rectangular inner bailey and a semi-circular outer bailey with three ditches on the North side. This accords with Speed's representation which also includes a large shell keep. Leland wrote:-

The Castle stands hard by the West Gate and hath a large keep. The area of the residue is very large and bulwarks of earth be made before the Castle Gate'.

'T.C.R.' gives the measurements of the inner bailey inside its walls as 'East to west 486 feet' and 'from North to south 324 feet' giving an area of just over 3½ acres. The walls of the inner bailey were repaired in 1255 and 1258. Fig. 3 (plan) shows the West, and portions of the East wall (double lines). A section of the South wall with a ruined bastion (B) 'in diameter 20 feet by 15 feet and 18 feet high' and the West wall, with a pointed postern gate, are illustrated. Serjeantson's plan shows part of the South wall destroyed by St. Andrew's Road and no eastern remains. A photograph of the West wall and gate has survived (V.C.H.). The wall itself was demolished, but the gate may be seen in a wall outside the present station.

The North gate was the main entrance to the inner bailey. It is shown on Speed's representation and Serjeantson places a jamb on the East side of St. Andrew's Road. A barbican was added but in 1323 was in ruinous condition (Survey).

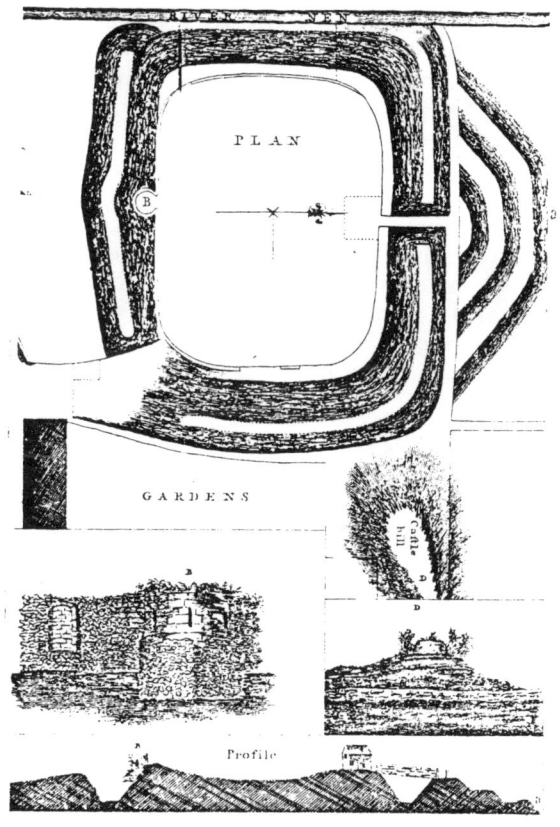

3. The Castle Ruins from 'The Gentleman's Magazine' October 1800

The King's Houses

Serjeantson suggests the shell keep lay in the North-west corner of the inner bailey. The 1863 excavation revealed a considerable domestic block inside the South wall. It had sustained serious fire damage which suggests these were the royal buildings - the Great Hall, two principal chambers and lower chapel - listed as requiring repairs in the 1323 survey - taken after fire had damaged much of the castle in 1318.

The King's living quarters had moved from the Keep to the 'Great Hall' by 1164. Accounts of Henry II's confrontation with Thomas Becket reveal that this took place in a large hall with a central fire, the King's chambers, where he consulted with the clerics while Becket waited in the main hall, being 'upstairs'.

The 'modernisation' of the royal quarters commenced under King John who, in 1208 introduced glass and a bath. This trend was followed by his son, Henry III. From his alterations and repairs (Liberate Rolls) emerges a picture of the domestic quarters Edward and Eleanor inherited here.

The Hall was lit by 'large' windows and five small windows these being ordered in 1248. A window 'to shut and open' decorated with the images of 'Lazarus and Dives' (the poor and rich men in St. Luke's Gospel) was to be made on the North side (1252) opposite the King's desk (1253). Wainscott had been ordered 'over the King's seat' (1249) but this seat may have been replaced as a new chair was to be carved in accordance with verbal instructions and painted in 1269/70.

The Royal Apartments

The King and Queen's apartments in the hall block consisted of the King's chamber and wardrobe and the Queen's chamber and chapel. The latter were on the ground floor on the North side of the Hall. The entrance to her chamber was next to the 'Lazarus' window. Her chapel, which had replaced the Hall porch (1248), faced the chamber. The glass windows of both were protected by iron bars. The chamber was wainscotted (1244) and whitewashed (1260).

The King's chamber and wardrobe were probably still on the upper floor. Two glass windows had been 'newly made' in the chamber in 1270/1 at a cost of 44 shillings, just 6 shillings less than the priest's annual salary. The wardrobe had a window and a fire-place.

The King's chapel was separate from the Hall, a wall stretching between it and the inner bailey wall and the walls about it being crenellated in 1252. It was to be provided with 'sufficient books and ornaments' (1247), a missal worth 2 marks in 1252, and repaired in 1248 and in 1259/60. A room, a privy chamber, for the chaplains was built 'against the doorway of the Hall'.

References to a dovecote, garden and garden gate, walled deer-park, regular and comparatively large shipments of wine, chambers in the 'New Tower' and the large number of dishes (4,000) stored there, all betoken a growing domestic use of the Castle throughout the 13th. century. It did, however, retain its jail, repaired in 1260.

The decline of the Castle

After the fire damage of 1318 the castle declined. In the 1323 survey it was estimated that £702 was required to repair the domestic buildings and £395. 6s. 8d. to restore the Castle's defences. There is nothing to suggest such repairs were instigated. In 1320, £3. 6s. 8d. was allocated 'for covering the houses' and, three years later further repairs 'up to £20' were allowed.

There may have been some restoration at the outbreak of the 17th. century Civil War, but, after that, the site and Castle remains fell into private hands. The 'Gentleman's Magazine' drawing shows the outer bailey between the West wall and the River Nene planted with trees, a barn 'belonging to the farm-yard' and no remains other than the walls and wall bastion in the inner bailey.

From 1863-1880 the area was levelled to accommodate the Castle Railway Station and buildings. The station was rebuilt 1963-4 and the River Nene diverted.

Edward and Eleanor at Northampton Castle

Eleanor's Wardrobe Accounts show she was at Northampton with Edward from August 21st. - 29th. 1290, when the final details for the marriage of their son Edward with Margaret of Scotland were being discussed with the Council. This was the usual royal residence in Northampton and there is no reason to believe that the King and main Court officials would stay anywhere else during the night or nights the Queen's Cortège stopped at Northampton.

Northampton in 1290 (Town)
Churches in 1290

Leland counted 7 parish churches within the walls of Northampton. When Bishop Hugh Wells confirmed to St. Andrew's Priory 'all the churches of Northampton' eight churches were named in the Town. (Monasticum Vol.5 p. 191). Leland's St. Katherine's Chapel was not included. It was reputedly built in the 14th. century for the burial of plague victims. ('K' on Speed's map). Of the churches listed four are shown by Speed - Holy Sepulchre (D), St. Giles' (X), All Saints' (R) and St. Peter's (S) and survive, inevitably altered, to-day. Full accounts of the architectural histories of these churches may be found in the Victoria County History for Northampton shire and Pevsner.

Holy (St.) Sepulchre

The original Church of the Holy Sepulchre was founded in Jerusalem on the supposed site of Christ's burial by St. Helena the mother of Constantine the Great. This church was enlarged and after 1118 became associated with the Knights Templars.

In Northampton the Church of the Holy Sepulchre was founded in the early 12th. century - if by Simon Senlis I before 1111 - this Eastern style of architecture then being popular. It was superseded by the Gothic and many round and apsidal end churches were altered accordingly. Holy Sepulchre, Northampton is one of the 4/5 round churches left in this Country.

It may be found in the North of the Town on Church Lane, inside the old North Gate (Campbell Street).

St. Giles

This Church stands within the old East wall (York Road) on St. Giles' Street. A cruciform church with a central tower was commenced c.1120. This was the St. Egidu of Bishop Hugh Wells of Lincoln's charter.

During the 13th. century the chancel was re-built, being extended in length and on the North. Work was started on a southern extension but discontinued, possibly because of fears for the tower, which was then strengthened. The tower did not fall until 1613 when it damaged the nave, necessitating some rebuilding.

The Church was restored in the 19th. century. Remnants of 12th. and 13th. century work are found in the tower, chancel and West door.

All Saints' (Hallow's)

The West end of St. Giles' Street runs into George Row. Between this and Mercers' Row, in the middle of the old Town, lies All Saints.

The original Church was in existence well before 1235 when Bishop Hugh Wells offered indulgences (forgiveness of sins) to anyone who worked on repairs. The core of the present tower is believed to date from the 12th. century and a crypt below the chancel from the 13th. century (Pevsner).

Leland found All Saints' 'the principal Church' in the

'heart of the Town . . . large and well-built'. Speed shows a cruciform church with a 'central' tower, in a rectangular walled yard, situated on the South side of the 1610 Market Place. Henry Lee, Town Clerk in 1675 reported that the Church was 'as large as some cathedrals'.

This structure was virtually destroyed in the Town fire of 1675. Much of the present Church is a late 17th. century re-build.

At the Dissolution (1537) the advowsons (right to appoint the incumbant) of Holy Sepulchre, St. Giles' and All Saints' which had been held by St. Andrew's Priory, were sold to Sir Thomas Smith (Monasticum).

St. Peter's

St. Peter's stands in Marefair, south-east of the Castle site. According to Pevsner it was founded 1150 or a little later. The Victoria County History dates the chancel and nave arcades, the tower arch and part of the clerestory walls c. 1150-1175. Pevsner also notes a mid 12th. century sepulchral slab.

When Bishop Hugh Wells confirmed St. Peter's as a St. Andrew's church, this was disputed by Henry III and in 1253 an inquiry was held. The jury found that the church had been held by Henry II (1154-1189) but, after that it had passed to the Priory. Henry III recovered the church by paying St. Andrew's a yearly pension.

It would appear the medieval Church was larger than the present one, the nave having extended 10 feet (V.C.H.) further West 'with a tower beyond'. When Gilbert Scott was renovating the East end, he was informed that the foundations extended from the (present) tower westwards (Arch. Journal XXXV p.417).

During the 13th. century St. Peter's was a large royal Church. A ramp from the Castle onto Black Lion Hill, shown on the Castle plans and by Speed, would have given access to both the West Bridge and St. Peter's. Provided the main Cortège stayed at the Castle, either one of the Castle chapels or St. Peter's could have conveniently accommodated the Queen's body.

The Lost Churches

St. Michael's, St. Mary's, St. Gregory's and St. Edmund's were the other four churches named in Bishop Hugh Well's Confirmation. The first was in Cock Lane (V.C.H.) which is shown to run between Abington Street and Lady's Lane in the 1810 map and would now be covered by the Grosvenor Centre. St. Michael's merged with Holy Sepulchre. St. Mary by the Castle and St. Gregory's were given to All Saints'. St. Mary's Street runs between Horsemarket and Chalk Lane. St. Gregory's was converted into a school. St. Edmund's was absorbed by St. Giles' at the Reformation, which would place it on the East side of the Town.

Gilds and Gild Hall

Most of Northampton Gilds were the product of the 14th. century, but, in a Gild document of 1388 it was stated that one, the Gild of St. Mary had been established before 1272. It was to supply three chaplains and was established at All Saints' which suggests St. Mary's had been amalgamated by 1388.

The Gild Hall, as at Lincoln, was used for legal proceedings being identified in 1385 as 'the place where the Mayor and Bailiffs hold their pleas'. A 'common hall', probably for a similar purpose, was in use 100 years earlier.

There was a town prison by 1253. No 13th. century houses survived the Fire of 1675.

The Friaries of Northampton

Leland places four friaries Franciscan, Carmelite, Dominican and Austin all inside the Town walls. There had also been a Friary of the Penance of Jesus Christ (Sack) and there is an early reference to 'five Franciscan nuns'.

The Friary of the Penance of Jesus Christ

On January 10th. 1304 Edward held an inquiry to discover whether it would be predjudicial to him or others to grant a messuage, which Eleanor had given to the Friars of Sack, Northampton, to Master Ralph de Haule, the parson of St. Peter's. This property was then in the King's hands so the Friary had disappeared before 1304, having been subjected to the closure order of 1274.

The Victoria County History of Northamptonshire sites their house in the South-east quarter of the Town between Dern Gate and 'Dandeline's Court' (unidentified) in 1274/5.

The Franciscan Friars

Tanner (Notitia Monastica) claimed the Grey Friars first settled in the Parish of St. Giles (i.e. outside the East Gate of the Town) but they afterwards moved North of the Market Place, a siting given by Leland - 'a little beyond the chief market place, almost flat North.' This is the only friary shown on Speed's map where it lies slightly East of North of the market (H).

The Friars embarked on a second building programme in the 1270's which may be indicative of when they moved within the Town walls. Possibly to assist this building,

Edward provided them with a horse and cart. Unfortunately this gift caused the death of Richard de Lilleford and was seized as compensation. Leland claimed Greyfriars was 'the best built and largest' of all the Northampton friaries.

It was dissolved in 1546 and granted to Richard Taverner (Tanner) although Leland in 1534-42 had reported 'the site and ground it stood on belonged to the City'.

In the 1972 excavations the remains of a 'double vaulted medieval structure 30 feet by 120 feet and a floor area of glazed tiles' were discovered South of Lady's Lane (Pevsner). The position would suggest these were remnants of the Franciscan Friary.

The Carmelite Friary

Leland placed the White Friars 'a little above the Grey Friars' probably using 'above' in its contemporary meaning of further North than. This Friary is not shown on Speed's map nor is a space between the Grey Friary and the Church of the Holy Sepulchre. In reality, there is suffficent area between Holy Sepulchre and the Old Market to have housed both friaries.

In 1278 the Carmelites requested permission to enclose a portion of the Town wall that adjoined their close and a 'noisome and muddy way' between the Friary and the wall was mentioned, which places the Friary near the North-east section of the Town wall i.e. Upper Mounts. In 1846 excavations revealed foundations of what was probably the Carmelite church under the present Kerr Street (V.C.H.). This church was dedicated to the Virgin Mary, 'Our Lady' so that the Friary could reasonably be placed 'between Newland, Lady's Lane and Upper Mounts.

Dugdale (Monasticum) names Simon Mountfort and Thomas Chitwood as the Founders. Provided the former were the leader of the Barons' Rebellion, as would appear, Simon the younger having no opportunity and the Beaudesert (Warwickshire) Montfords both being called Peter, the Carmelites were established before 1265, when Simon was killed at the Battle of Evesham.

The Austin Friary

Leland placed the Austin Friary 'in the West side of the street by the South Gate, hard against St. John's Hospital'. As part of this 12th. century hospital has survived (Q on Speed's map) it is possible to site the Austins on Bridge Street, somewhere between Angel Street and Victoria Promenade.

The house became associated with the Longville family

of Wolverton during the 14th. century and it has been claimed that Sir John Longville founded the Friary in 1323. According to the Victoria County History there were references to the Friary in local deeds between 1275 and 1290. This would make it one of the earliest English Austin establishments.

At the Dissolution (July 1540) the site was granted to Robert Dighton of Stirton, Lincs.

The Dominican Friary

Bridges gave John Babington as either this Friary's founder or early benefactor. Building activity continued over 67 years, the first reference being in 1233 when timber was granted from the Warwickshire Forest of Kenilworth. The Church was roofed in 1246, but the following year the Friars acquired more land and extended the church, roofing the extension in 1249. In 1258 study rooms were added.

In 1279 they followed the usual procedure of installing running water, building a conduit to carry it from a well, Flexwell at Kingsthorpe, given to them by Queen Eleanor. (V.C.H.).

The Friary was placed by Leland 'in the street where the Horse Market is kept once a week'. Horse-market Street still exists. There is some disagreement over the side on which the Friary lay. The V.C.H. supports Serjeantson's positioning on the East side to Gold Street on the South, claiming Dr. Cox's placing, in his map in the Borough Records, incorrect. In John Britton's 'Plan of Northampton' from 'Beauties of England and Wales' 1810, a Friary, labelled 'Grey Friars' is shown on the West side of Horse Market, between what is now Castle Street and Bath Street. It is possible remnants of a friary could be found there in 1810 and were incorrectly labelled. This position is attractive for the Black Friary as it coincides with a blank on Speed's map and would link the Dominican's conduit with Scarlet Well and Cold Bath.

The Friary was dissolved in 1539 being granted to William Ramsden.

The Religious Houses outside the Walls

Three monasteries lay outside the Town walls - the Abbey of St. James, and the two Cluniac houses, St. Andrew's in the North and De La Prie in the South.

The Abbey of St. James

Leland placed this house of Austin Canons 'a little distant from the extreme part of the western suburb. 'Bridges gave a contemporary (18th.century) description of the site, the Church and churchyard covering two acres and the Abbey desmesne lying on both sides of the road to Banbury.

'Going down to the Abbey is a causey called Cut Throat Lane with an old wall (Leland's high, fair and large wall that 'compass the whole site of the House') on the left. In a close adjoining was a mill, supplied by a spring now called the Abbey Spring. In this close was kept St. James' fair and here is supposed to have stood the Abbey itself'.

The way to St. James' abbey was across the River Nene by the Castle Bridge. The Grand Union Canal and modern development have eliminated that first part of the old Banbury Road referred to by Bridges. It can be reached via the A45 and the B4525. The Abbey site is remembered in St. James' End (a division for tax purposes) St. James' Road, Mill Road, and Business Park - perhaps an echo of the medieval Fair.

The first Austin Canons in England were probably at St. Botolph's Colchester in 1107. The label of Austin Canons regular covered a wide variety of religious establishments. 'No systematic attempt to organise the canons as a whole into an order was made until after the Fourth Lateran Council of 1215'. (Lawrence "Medieval Monasticism").

The Abbey's Church was rebuilt 1290-1310. It was not directly on the Cortége route so that though prestigious and used for State occasions during the following century it was unlikely to have played a major role in December 1290.

Two Cluniac Monasteries

The monastery of Cluny was founded in 910 by William, Count of Avergne and Duke of Aquitaine. Cluny is a town in Burgundy, France, lying in the Department of Saone-et-Loire and on the left bank of the River Grosne. Part of the South transept of the Abbey Church and, a few fragments of sculpture remain (Clark). It was to the Abbot of Cluny Edward wrote after Eleanor's final funeral, requesting prayers for her soul.

Cluniac monks followed the Benedictine rule. Their Order was introduced to England under William the Conqueror, the first foundation being at Barnstaple and the second at Lewes in 1077.

St. Andrew's Priory

On the evidence of Ingulph, Bridges and Tanner favour an early St. Andrew's, prior to the Senlis foundation. There is a reference to an early house adjoining the Chapel of St. Martin, in a later Patent Roll (1348), so St. Andrew's was either founded or re-founded by Simon Senlis I and his wife Matilda. This must have occurred after their marriage, which could not have taken place before 1085. Simon's connections with the Cluniac house at La Charité sur Loire, where he was buried, probably inspired the foundation. The first monks at St. Andrew's came from La Charité. St. Andrew's was administered by Priors under the authority of the mother house. Perhaps because of this, the Priors were often abroad. In 1288 Prior Bernard was away so long he was considered to have deserted the House and was replaced by Odo, who was Prior in 1290.

In spite of their claim to 'all the churches of Northampton' the visitations of 1262, 1275/6 and 1279 all revealed the monks were in debt. Like other large monastic establishments, St. Andrew's carried the heavy financial burden of universal hospitality. Thomas Becket and his train were appointed lodgings at St. Andrew's for Henry II's council of 1164. Becket's complaint over the part occupation of the Priory by William de Courcy suggests the quarters were considered prestigious, housing the higher ranks of the Castle overspill. It is quite likely the Priory played the same role in 1290, accommodating part of the Queen's Cortège.

Leland placed St. Andrew's at the North end of the Town, hard by the North Gate. The large chapel he reported outside that gate was probably the conventual church. The walled monastery is shown on Speed's map at 'B' and the Priory mill at 'A'. Stone coffins and fragments found on the site are housed in the Museum.

Tanner states the site was granted to Sir Thomas Smith under Edward VI.

The Abbey of De La Prie

South of the Town, on the London Road, a house of cluniac nuns, known as De La Prie (in the fields) or St. Mary's de Pratis (1246) was established by Simon Senlis II during the reign of King Stephen. (Tanner).

In 1246 King Henry III gave the Abbey a silver cup for the celebration of the Eucharist costing 10 marks (Liberate Rolls).

After some altercation, Margery de Wolaston, the sub-prioress, succeeded Emma Malory as Abbess in 1282. She remained in office until her death in 1296/7.

In 1542 the Abbey and lands were granted to John Marsh (Patent). They later passed to the Tate family. A new house was built on the site. Some remnants of the Abbey were still standing in 1720 (Bridges).

The Tate house was restored in 1957/8, after a public appeal, and is now in use as the Northamptonshire Record Office.

Hospitals

There were two hospitals in 1290. The Hospital of St. John the Baptist for the poor stood on Bridge Street between St. John's Street and Victoria Promenade, just inside the South Gate of the medieval Town ('Q' on Speed's map). At the dissolution the site covered 3½ acres. St. Leonard's lazar house was outside the walls, at Cotton End across the River Nene south along the London Road.

St. John the Baptist

Leland gave William St. Clare, Archdeacon of Northampton (died 1168) as the founder of this Hospital. A Master, monks and brethren are mentioned in the Pope Nicholas tax of 1291.

The 13th. century hospital had a church (re-built 1309) a burial ground (enlarged 1286) and was likely to have had a hall with a central aisle, beds down each side and rooms above for the monks. At some time, the Master was provided with a separate house. A photograph exists of the structure demolished in the 19th. century.

The Victoria County History dates the surviving hall from the early 14th. century. This hall, with the 14th. century chapel, both altered and restored, are now in use as a Catholic Church.

St. Leonard's

William the Conqueror and Richard le Stafford have both been named as the founders of this Hospital for lepers. It housed a Master and a mixed community. The Chapel and churchyard also served the inhabitants of Cotton. The hospital was demolished in 1823 (V.C.H.).

The Cortège in Northampton - a suggested route

Entering from Abington Abbey by the East gate of the Town, the Cortège would have passed St. Giles' Church. Abington Street would have brought the Court to the central market square and All Saints'. Here the bier could have rested so that the chief citizens might be witnesses to the Queen's death, the people might mourn and offer prayers for her soul, and dole be distributed.

From the Market the way to the Castle would depend on where the Queen's body was to stay. If the Castle chapel were the venue, the markets would have been crossed in a north-west direction to the main castle entrance. If the Queen were to stay before the altar of St. Peter's, the line of Gold Street would be followed. After the body had been received, the Court could enter the Castle, unladen, by the southern entrance.

On the morning of December 9th. after the King had signed a writ, the Cortège would have left by Bridge Street, past St. John's Hospital, through the South Gate, past St. Leonard's Hospital to the Abbey of De La Prie. Here the cross site was selected.

The Northampton Cross

This is the second of the three crosses which have survived (*fig. 4*). It lies on the East side of the A508, just before a large roundabout outside of the wall of the Record Office (De La Prie). It is possible to leave a car in a small road opposite.

4. The Northampton Cross
(Drawing by Jill Sturman)

Celia Fiennes passed the Cross on her way from Northampton to Stoney Stratford, in 1697. She described it as 'all stone .. twelve steps which run round it. Above that is the stone carved finely, and there are four large niches about the middle - in each the statue of some Queen at length which encompasses it with other carvings as garnish and so it rises less and less to the like a tower or piramidy'.

The Northampton or Hardingstone Cross has been renovated at least twice since Celia Fiennes saw it. The earlier restoration is recorded by a plaque, which states it was carried out by:-

'The Honorable Assembly of Judges in 1713.. in which year it had nearly fallen down by reason of age'.

The Cross was seen to signify 'an everlasting memory of conjugal love'. The second restoration was in 1986.

Only 10 steps are now visible, but it is possible others lie beneath the turf. The base is octagonal and some remnants suggest Purbeck marble was used in its construction. There are, as Celia Fiennes claimed, four full-length statues of Eleanor. The top of the cross has been left broken. (*see fig. 4*).

It is impossible to cost the Northampton Cross accurately from the accounts of the Queen's executors, owing to lumped payments. The progress of the construction may be traced.

The first payment was made during Michaelmas (Autumn) Term 1290 to John de Bello (Bataille-Battle) cementarius, and his associates. This first payment was specifically for work on the Northampton cross, but, in the Spring of 1291 he is paid for work on the crosses of Northampton and St. Alban's and, after Easter, for these crosses in association with a Symon of Pabeham, a cementarius.

Payments were then also commenced to Robert of Corf for marble hoods, rods and rings for the cross at Northampton amongst others, and to William of Hibernia (the Imagemaker) for images made for Northampton and 'elsewhere'.

In the Autumn of 1291, John de Bello was working on crosses at Dunstable and Stoney Stratford in addition to those at Northampton and St. Alban's, and, in Spring 1292, Woburn was added to the list. William of Hibernia took over the manufacture of the marble rods, rings and hoods, as well as the images of the Queen. These were made in London and, after Easter William de Bernak, cementarius, brought four images, rods and hoods 'all the way' from London to Northampton.

After August 1st. John de Bello received a payment for 'work done in stone' at Northampton, entered under 'cross' and, in the Autumn, he received a final payment for his work on the Cross and a fee for supervising the scaffolding and the lifting into position of the Queen's images.

Two Roads to Stoney Stratford

To-day, two major roads run from Northampton to the Roman/Medieval High Road, Watling Street (A5). The A43 (T) follows a south-westerly route to Towcester, the Lactodorum (Golden Milk) of the Romano-Britons. The A508 runs South, through Yardley Gobion to a roundabout, where the present A5 diverges from the line of Watling Street in order to by-pass Stoney Stratford. Both roads connect Domesday manors, so are likely to approximate to established ways.

The A43 route, by which the Cortège enetered Northampton, would have crossed the Town North-east to South-west, leaving by the West (Castle) Bridge. The A508 is now diverted from the Town centre, but the North-South line, leaving by the South Bridge, may still be traced. If these roads were separate lines of travel, only the A508 route would accommodate the Cortège stop at De La Prie Abbey for the selection of the Cross site. The route to Towcester, being shorter, had the advantage of offering swifter access to the King's Highway, passing through the Domesday manors of Milton Maslor, Blisworth, Hulcote, and Easton Neston. The A508 passes De La Prie and the Domesday manors of Hardingstone, Collingtree, Courteenhall, Roade, and Grafton Regis. The old road may have run from Grafton Regis to join Watling Street at Potterspury. Yardley Gobion is not a Domesday manor.

The King Leaves the Cortège

At some time after signing the writ at Northampton on December 9th. and before the cross site selection at Dunstable the King left the Cortège, to join it again at St. Alban's, where he signed a writ on December 13th.

Certain factors favour a separation on Watling Street, at, or before, Stratford. The reduction of the Cortège at this point would have rationalized stops at Stratford and Woburn where the accommodation in the 13th. century would appear to have been limited. Even if the first part of the journey from Northampton had been slowed down, due to accompanying the Cortège c.10 miles to Potterspury, the remaining c. 37 miles to St. Alban's would not have presented an impossible journey for a group of horsemen on a straight major road.

Trouble at St. Alban's.

Roger de Norton, the Abbot of St. Alban's had died on November 3rd. whereupon the King's Escheator, Malcolm de Harle, demanded property which he accounted the Abbot's, but the Prior, John de Marius, claimed belonged to the Abbey. In response to the Prior's appeal, Edward promised moderation. Malcolm de Harle's seizure of the property was the subject of a writ sent from Rufford, by the King on November 14th.

The Prior had appointed December 9th. as the day for the election of the new Abbot. John de Berkhamstead was chosen on that day. Although St. Alban's answered only to Rome and the King had no legal authority over the monks' choice, the Abbey was dependant on royal favour and it is possible the new Abbot was to be presented to, and approved by, the King, before he left for Rome to receive his pallium from the Pope.

These two matters would have required the King's presence at St. Alban's Abbey, and were probably his reasons for leaving the Cortège after Northampton. It would appear, from the Dunstable cross site selection, the Cortège was left in the capable hands of the King's friend and Chancellor, Robert Burnell.

PART VII
Stoney Stratford, Woburn, Toddington and Dunstable

Stratford

In the accounts of Queen Eleanor's executors the cross is at 'Stratford' in the Autumn of 1291 and at 'Stonistratford' in the Spring of 1292, suggesting that, by then, the single settlement of Stratford on both sides of the Great Ouse river, was dividing into the present 'Old Stratford' and Stoney Stratford.

Stoney Stratford

A bridge across the Great Ouse carried Watling Street from Old Stratford into Stoney Stratford. It was recorded in 1240 and probably replaced the original ford. The area was marshy and, according to Camden, subject to violent Winter flooding. Speed refers to Watling Street as an ancient causeway, and a reference to a causeway by the bridge in 1240 suggests that here the Street was raised.

Four Views of Stoney Stratford

According to Dugdale (Monasticum) in 1240 the hospital chapel (and therefore at some time almost certainly the hospital) of St. John stood on the causeway by the bridge at Stoney Stratford.

A survey from the reign of Henry VIII refers to the Swan Inn, the market square and 'Brotherhood House'.

Camden found the Town 'of a considerable largeness, beautified with two churches'. He also saw the Eleanor Cross in situ.

Celia Fiennes (1697) coming to the Town from Northampton via Hardingstone as Eleanor's Cortège had done, discovered:-

'a little place built all of stone, the manufactory of this part of the country for bone-lace, with all the inhabitants working at lace-making sitting all along the street as thick as can be'.

It would appear that even in the 16th. and 17th. centuries little of medieval Stoney Stratford had survived.

There was further destruction in 1742 when a fire consumed most of the East side of the Town.

Overnight Stay

The only place recorded in these descriptions which might have accommodated the reduced Cortège was the Brotherhood House. This belonged to Bradwell Priory. The Benedictine Priory itself stood c. 2miles further on the route, along Watling Street, 'on the extreme part of the Parish of Wolverton, bordering on the Town or Parish of Bradwell.' It seems to have been the only sizeable convent in the vicinity of Stoney Stratford. In the absence of further evidence the Priory and its Brotherhood House offer the only suitable stopping places in the Stoney Stratford area for the Cortège on the night of December 9th. 1290.

From a document of the reign of Henry VIII, quoted in 'Monasticon, ' Bradwell then appeared a substantial Priory with a gateway, courtyard, hall, cloisters, chapel and dorter (monks' dormitory). It had been founded in 1155 by the Lord of the manor of Wolverton. In 1280 the Prior had been Robert of Ramsey.

Although it was claimed in the 1846 edition of Monasticon that the Priory site was occupied by a farmhouse and there were no remains, ruins are shown on the O/S map Landranger 152 SP 826 395.

The Cross at Stoney Stratford

Camden placed the Cross 'in the middle of the Town'. Browne Willis, in his 'Records of Buckinghamshire' states William Hartley remembered the base of the Cross 'at the lower end of the Town, by Horse Shoe Inn'. A plaque to mark the site has been placed between numbers 157 and 159 High Street (Watling Street).

As the cross at Stoney Stratford was one of five constructed under the supervision of John de Bello, it is impossible to cost it accurately. The first payment to name this cross was recorded in the Autumn of 1291. At the end of Hilary Term (Spring) 1292, Radulpho de Cyestria (Ralph of Chichester) was given £5, in part payment of £14, for 5 rods, 5 hoods, and 5 rings of marble bought for four crosses, including that of Stoney Stratford. By Trinity (after Whitsun) John de Bello had moved into the 'operations' stage, which appears to have been concerned with raising and fixing the Queen's images. His final payment, of one mark, for the four 'Watling Street' crosses (Stoney Stratford, Woburn, Dunstable and St. Alban's) was made in the Spring of 1293.

The Appearance of the Cross

There is no separate record of payment for images for the Stratford cross in the accounts. These appear to have been bought 'from the book' of William of Hibernia's London workshop. However, the purchase of rods, hoods and rings specifically for this cross, suggests it did bear images of the Queen. According to Camden it was 'adorned with the arms of England, Castile and Leon and the County of Ponthieu'. The extended survival of the base would suggest this cross was raised on substantial steps. Camden considered it 'not very splendid' but may have been comparing it with the more expensive London crosses, or it is possible the cross was in poor condition, when he saw it.

Fate

Nothing of this Cross is known to remain. Celia Fiennes does not mention it in 1697 and the fact that William Hartley, a man of 'nearly 80' in 1735 remembered only the base still standing suggests it disappeared during the Civil War or inter-regnum.

Stoney Stratford to Woburn

Watling Street rejoins the A5 a mile after Feeny Stratford, having crossed the River Ouzel. It continued to Little Brickhill where the Cortège could have left Watling Street and taken the way to Woburn Abbey. The whole journey would have covered about nine miles - less if the Cortège started from Bradwell.

Woburn Cross

Although Woburn Cross does not appear to have been recorded in situ and its precise position and fate are unknown, it was listed by Stowe (Survey of London) and is referred to by name six times in the accounts of the Queen's executors, being one of John de Bello's five crosses.

The Cross is first mentioned in the Spring Term of 1292. It was probably completed before the end of that year, although it is named in John de Bello's final payment made in Spring 1293.

Woburn Abbey

If the overnight stop for Sunday December 10th. were at Woburn, the only possible accommodation would have been at the Cistercian Abbey. It had been founded c.1145 by Hugh de Bolebec, tenant of the manor of Woburn at that time. A colony of monks was sent to inhabit it from Fountains Abbey.

From c. 1183-1225 Woburn was involved in a protracted dispute with St. Alban's Abbey and Dunstable Priory over the advowson of Chesham Church. In 1232 the Abbey, being in financial difficulties, was granted money from the Subsidy. By 1234 the community was virtually destitute. The Abbot was re-deployed and the monks dispersed to other religious houses. Dugdale (Monasticum) assumed the Abbey was closed down. It did, however, survive.

The Prior of Dunstable granted the Abbey a mill. In 1235 money collected for an Aid was lodged there and, in 1240, a canon from Dunstable, seeking to avoid the enforcement of Bishop Grosseteste of Lincoln's reforms, which included the celibacy of the priesthood, fled to Woburn. The Friday market and yearly fair granted in 1245 and a gift of land in Bishopgate, London, made by the Prior of St. Pancreas (undated) added to the Abbey's prosperity. The former were given at 'the Old Chapel of Woburn' which suggests the Abbey chapel may, by then, have been re-built. Leland claimed the Abbey had been founded by Isabel (Bolebec) the wife of Robert de Vere, Earl of Oxford. Although she would have been too young to have initiated the Abbey, she may have assisted in the re-vitalization of her Grandfather's (?) foundation. She died in 1244.

Little is known about the Abbey during the years 1245 to 1289, but it appears to have made a good recovery over that period. In 1289 and 1291 the Abbot was collecting debts owed to the Abbey. The assessment made in 1291 for Pope Nicholas' tax placed Woburn amongst the wealthiest convents in the Country, so that in 1290, it should have been capable of housing the Cortège.

The Fate of the Abbey

The Abbey stood about one mile East of Woburn village. It was surrendered in 1534/5 and in 1537 its last Abbot was hanged in the Abbey Park for having taken part in the 'Pilgrimage of Grace'. Woburn with all its possessions, together with two other Abbeys was granted to John Russell, a member of the new Tudor aristocracy.

A mansion built on the Abbey site was demolished, together with the remaining walls of the Abbey Church and Cloisters to make way for the present house built in 1746. Pevsner considers 'the cloister was probably where the courtyard between the three wings now is'.

Woburn to Dunstable

Any route from Woburn to Dunstable via Watling Street would have included that stretch of the High Road from Hockcliff to Dunstable which Camden described as 'a dirty road extreme troublesome to travellers in the Wintertime' and Celia Fiennes about a hundred years later, 'a sad road'. The lie of the land suggests this area had always been subject to flooding and may have been included in Edward's order for repairs to the roads through Dunstable in February 1285.

Watling Street could have been avoided if the route through Toddington were taken.

1. Partly demolished Priory Church at Dunstable

Toddington

This had been an important settlement pre-Domesday. An earthwork known as Conger Hill, 92 feet in diameter across the top (Pevsner) east of the church, may be a relique of this time.

Matthew Paris described a manor house there, built in the 13th. century by Paul Pever, courtier and servant to Henry III, who died in 1252, with 'such grandeur, such a chapel, such lodgings, with other houses of stone covered with lead, and surrounded with such avenues and parks that it raised astonishment in the beholders'. It is not certain where this house stood. The 16th. century manor house, which Camden recorded as 'lately' built by Henry, Lord Cheney (Toddington passed by marriage from the Pevers to the Cheneys in 1530) was on the site of the present manor, North-west of the village, on the way from Woburn.

Toddington possessed a market square, now attractively grassed over, and a market cross, sometimes mistaken for Eleanor's. The Church of St. George stands by the market square. Pevsner dates the South transcept, double piscina (basin for washing communion and mass vessels) mid 13th. century and the crossing arches, blind arcading inside the tower and south doorway, all 13th. century.

Badly damaged monuments of members of both the Pever and Cheney families may be seen in the South Transcept. One is the effigy of an early 14th. century knight, and may have represented Paul Pever's grandson, John, Lord at Toddington in 1290, who died in 1315. John Pever was married to Marie de Pecquigny, Eleanor's third cousin. Paul Pever's heart was buried at Toddington but his body at London (V.C.H.). It seems likely the Cortège would have visited Toddington and the House of Pevers, which, if Matthew Paris did not exaggerate was capable of offering overnight accommodation.

St. George's stands 485 feet above sea-level, but the drop to Watling Street, as well as the Hockcliff to Dunstable stretch, could have been avoided if the Cortège had gone by way of the Domesday settlements of Chalgrave and Houghton (Regis) to Icknield Way (A505). The nearest equivalent would be the A5120 but this is blocked from the A505 by industrial development and the modern traveller is forced back onto Watling Street.

Dunstable Priory stood at the junction of these two major medieval ways.

Dunstable

The medieval settlement of Dunstable seems to have resulted from a deliberate colonization by Henry I, about his palace of Kingsbury. Camden claims this was 'to prevent the mischief of one, Dun, a famous robber, and his gang'. Henry established the Priory opposite his palace, and granted the settlement a market (staple) and fair. In 1204 King John gave the palace to the Priory.

Dunstable Priory

Behind the High Street, a short way along Church Street (A505), may be found the reduced priory church of St. Peter and a sports field on which the conventual buildings of the old Priory stood.

This Priory of Augustine canons was founded c.1131, and its church consecrated in 1213 by Hugh Wells, Bishop of Lincoln. Much of the latter collapsed in 1222, destroying the Prior's house. Re-building started immediately. In 1273 the North aisle was restored by the parishioners.

The Church came to be shared, the Canons using the Nave, South aisle and, inevitably, the chancel, from which the lay public were excluded. As the population increased, the villagers requested, and were granted, the use of the Nave (1392). This was fortunate as, at the Dissolution, parish churches were spared, and though the Canons' portion of the Church, together with the conventual buildings, was demolished, the Town's nave and aisle have survived. This accounts for the Church's unbalanced external appearance (*see fig. 1*). The attractive interior with its Norman and Early English features, indicate the quality of what was destroyed.

It was in the Lady Chapel at Dunstable Priory Church that Cranmer pronounced the marriage of Henry VIII and Katherine of Aragon null and void on May 23rd. 1533.

2. Reconstruction of the Church

The Conventual Buildings

At the front of the Church of St. Peter, a 15th. century gateway leads onto the convent site/recreation ground. There is no evidence from excavation, but, in the rolls, the usual components of a large 13th. century convent are recorded:- a gate, courtyard, Prior's house, refectory, dormitory, infirmary and chapel, brew and bake houses, workshops, a great stable and guest house, houses for pigeons and craftsmen, noticeably carpenters and wheelwrights! A conjectural re-construction of the Church and Monastery has been made by Mr. F.A. Fowler (*see figs. 2 & 3*).

The Dominican Friary

The Friars Preachers or Black Friars settled in Dunstable c.1259. From the 'Annales of the Prior' it appears they came 'sorely against the will of the Prior and canons, but, the Friars being patronized by the Court, it was vain for others to resist'.

Tanner claims the Dominican Friary was

'in a field of Mrs. Fossey's, near her house situated West of a pond in South Street'. As, according to Camden, 'Dunstable had four streets answering to the four quarters of the World, and, because of the dryness of the soil, each one has a public pond' this would have been a precise siting at the time, placing the Friary on the West side of the present High Street. It is remembered in Friars' Walk.

Overnight Stay

Being on Watling Street and Icknield Way, the Priory was responsible for the entertainment of many travellers, particularly those passing to and from London. No doubt the 'great stable' was well used and the wheelwrights kept busy. A 13th. century vaulted chamber, now in 'Priory House' was part of the Priory guest house. Edward and Eleanor stayed at the Priory in 1275, Edward the next year and, in 1277, a special room for the King was commenced next to the Prior's. It would appear Edward did not stay there again.

The Priory analyst makes it clear that the Cortège stayed one night at the Priory, which received gifts of two precious cloths (baudekyns) and 80 pounds of wax or more.

Dunstable Cross

The analyst of Dunstable Priory's description of the selection of the cross site by Robert Burnell, implies the cross was in the market place. Camden wrote in 'Britannia' (1586)

'In the middle (of the Town) there is a cross, or rather a pillar, having engraven on it arms of England, Castile and Ponthieu and adorned with statues. It was built by King Edward I in memory of his Queen, Eleanor'. Rimmer (Ancient Stone Crosses) claims the cross was near 'the present' Town Hall.

Dunstable, the fourth of John de Bello's five crosses, shares its first payment with those for Northampton and Stoney Stratford, made in the Autumn of 1291. It is one of the crosses mentioned in Spring 1292 when payment was made to Ralph of Chichester for 5 rods, hoods and rings of marble. A payment 'after Easter' 1292 names Dunstable with Stoney Stratford and 'others'. After Whitsun, payments for 'operations' occupy the remainder of the year's accounts. Dunstable shares in the final settlement made for the four Watling Street crosses, in Spring 1293.

A Conjectural View of St Peter's Church and Monastery in the 14th Century

3. And of the Priory drawn by F.A. Fowler

Dunstable to St. Alban's

From Dunstable Watling Street (A5) ran past Markyate where a cell of St. Alban's had been established c.1145. The house later built on this site is known as The Cell. It is famous for its 'Wicked Lady' associations and stands in walled grounds on the corner of the A5 and B4540 just before Markyate village. After Friars' Wash, Watling Street passed through Redbourne, which is by-passed by the A5.

PART VIII
St. Alban's

St. Alban's
The Arrival of the Cortège

1. The River Ver at the 'Fighting Cocks'

Watling Street entered the ruined Romano-British town of Verulamium, which had stood on the River Ver, by the Chester (North-west) Gate, running approximately down what is now Gorhambury Drive. This was the route of Eleanor's Cortège. Passing the then buried remains of the Roman theatre, it came to the Church of St. Michael where, according to the Annales of St. Alban's and to Thomas Walsingham (Historia Anglicana) it was met by the whole convent in their copes (dress for processing).

Neither the King nor the Abbot are specifically mentioned in these accounts. Technically, there was no Abbot, as John de Berkhamstead was not installed until St. Alban's Day (June 22nd.) the following year. The writ dated at St. Alban's for December 13th. 1290 suggests that even were the King not there to greet the Cortège on its arrival on December 12th. he was present at St. Alban's when it departed for Waltham the following day.

Leaving the Church of St. Michael, which had been founded in 948 and still retains its Saxon nave and chancel, and 12th. century aisles, the procession would most conveniently have forded the River Ver near the present Fighting Cocks, where there is now a bridge. (*see fig.1.*). The ground rises noticeably to the Abbey from the River and the Cortège would have welcomed the Convent's help, at this point. (*see fig. 2 "Veralanium"*).

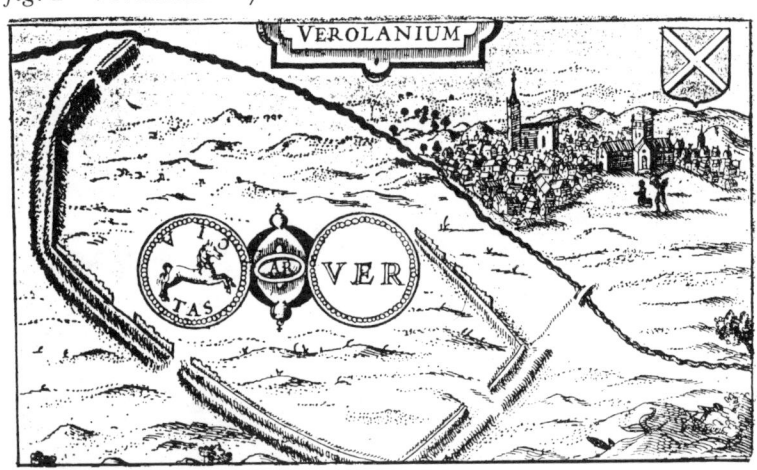

2. Speed's Pictorial Plan of 'Verolanium' and St. Alban's

Having entered the Abbey grounds through St. Germain's Gate, the procession would have passed the conventual buildings to reach the Abbey Church. The St. Alban's Chronicler (and Walsingham) record that 'the whole convent gathered before the High Altar (where the Queen, by implication, was laid) that night, and honored her with the Divine Offices, sacred vigil and prayers'.

St. Alban's Churches

St. Alban's Abbey

Bede tells how, in 301 A.D. during the persecution of Christians by the Emperor Diocletion, Alban, a Romano-Briton, sheltered Amphibalus, a Christian priest, and helped him to escape by taking his place. Alban then declared himself a Christian and was executed on a hill about 500 paces from the arena at Verulamium. Amphibalus was caught and put to death at Redbourn. Dr. John Morris of London University has demonstrated how the relevant persecution took place under Severus, which places the Saints' deaths around 209 A.D.

During the Saxon invasions, Alban's tomb was destroyed and his remains lost. Matthew Paris, a monk of St. Alban's, tells how Offa II, King of Mercia, miraculously recovered the martyr's body and established a monastery to house it.

After the Conquest, the Abbot, Paul, destroyed the Saxon Church and erected one in the style of St. Stephen's at Caen. This Norman church was consecrated in the presence of Henry I and his Queen Edith Matilda in 1116 (Anglo-Saxon Chronicle). The new Town, called St. Alban's, grew up to the North of the Monastery.

The Abbey Church in 1290

By 1290 the nave of Abbot Paul's church had been extended westwards giving a total length of 275½ feet a new West front had been completed and the East end was undergoing alterations which would eliminate Abbot Paul's five apses. Chapels dedicated to St. Andrew and St. Cuthbert had been built and at least five additional altars had been set up in the nave, where the reredos paintings may still be seen on the West faces of the piers. During the 13th. century a rood screen, with the rood (cross) and attendant figures of Mary and St. John had been made by the Colchester brothers. This was damaged when the nave roof fell in 1323.

The Abbey Reliques

What were held to be St. Alban's remains were housed in a coffer made by Anketil. This was enclosed in a shrine of gold and silver, decorated with jewels, the work of Master John the Goldsmith. On two sides of this shrine the acts of the Saint were depicted, on the third the Cross, St. Mary and

St. John, and, on the fourth, Mary enthroned. On the Saint's day and Ascension Day it was processed, supported by four monks. Henry III had given gifts of jewellery and rich hangings to this shrine. A 14th. century base, smashed at the Dissolution and restored under Gilbert Scott, may be seen in the Saint's Chapel.

By 1290, the Abbey had acquired a rib of St. Wulfstan, an arm of St. Jerome and a piece of the 'true' cross. A shrine made by the Colchester brothers and supposedly containing the remains of the Christian priest, Amphibalus, stood before the 13th. century rood screen. A replacement Shrine stands in the North Ambulatory.

The Abbey Church is now also St. Alban's Cathedral. (*see fig.3*).

3. Aerial view of St. Alban's Cathedral and Abbey Church

The Monastery

The Saxon monastery had accommodated nuns and monks but, in the first half of the 12th. century the nuns were removed to Sopwell. The reformed Norman Benedictine establishment laid emphasis on learning and selected its novices accordingly. Nicholas Brakspear, son of an Abbey tenant and the only Englishman to occupy the papal chair, failed to gain admission on academic grounds.

The monastery buildings lay on the South side of the Church. The 14th. century wall arcading of the North Cloister walk may still be seen on the outside wall of the present Cathedral, partly obscured by 19th. century buttresses.

A wall enclosed the Church and Convent, which, in 1290 was probably breeched by three gates. The 'Great Gatehouse' standing West of the Cathedral was constructed after 1290, but is believed to stand on the site of an earlier gate. As well as St. Germain's Gate, by the 'Fighting Cocks' there was a South-east gate, Holy Well Gate, remembered in Holywell Hill. The Waxhouse Gate, on the North-east, where candles were made and sold to pilgrims, is considered to be of a later date. It stands almost opposite the site of the St. Alban's Eleanor Cross.

The St. Alban's Eleanor Cross

Although the Cross at St. Alban's has not survived its position and fate are well documented in local records. Payments for its construction are recorded in the accounts of the Queen's executors.

It was situated across the High Street from the Cathedral and in front of the 15th. century curfew tower (*see fig. 4*). This was the South end of the medieval market place.

Stukeley shows the Cross on his plan of St. Alban's dated 1721, although the 'base in front of the Tower' was demolished in 1701, to make room for a market cross built in 1703. This cross was demolished in its turn (1810). A drinking fountain was erected on the site by Mrs. Worley in 1874 (V.C.H.)

No 'in situ' representation of this Cross is known. It was raised on steps, which appear to have survived its demise, and, on which, the High Sheriff was arrested, by Oliver Cromwell and his men, during the Inter regnum. In the accounts, it was the last of John de Bello's 'Watling Street' crosses. Payments made in conjunction with the cross at Northampton were recorded for the Spring and Autumn of 1291. It was one of the four crosses for which 5 rings, 5 rods and 5 hoods were purchased from Ralph of Chichester in the Spring of 1292 suggesting it bore images of the Queen.

After Whitsun 1292 it appears to have moved, with the other 'Watling Street' crosses, into the 'operations' stage and it shared with them the final payment made in Spring 1293.

A Second Route Change

From St. Alban's the most direct way into London would have been to continue along Watling Street and enter the City from the North-west, through New Gate. For some reason the Cortège returned to the Ermine Street (here the A10) route, thus increasing the distance by about 17 miles, moving into the vicinity of the River Lea and what would have been its flood plain (*see Route Map*).

The avoidance of a flood area was not therefore a reason for this route change. The most obvious reason was to include Waltham Abbey in the Cortège itinerary. This Abbey was associated with Kings Henry I, II and III, and the Abbot, Reginald, had been with Edward and Eleanor in Gascony in 1287. There was an indication that after Northampton, the Cortege was in no hurry to reach London; the four journeys prior to that Town having covered c.95 miles and the four following only 54 miles. The route diversion and visit to Waltham Abbey would have absorbed time, necessary if, for example, preparations for the London or Westminster funerals were incomplete.

4. The Cross Site

As a chapel to receive the Queen's heart at Black Friars, London had been paid for on February 18th. 1290, and painting about the Queen's tomb there on December 13th., it would appear the essentials for the interment of the Queen's heart were prepared. At Westminster Abbey Church, the Chapel of Edward the Confessor had already been used for the burial of Edward's father, but, as a payment for stone, delivered to the Church for the building of the Queen's tomb, was only made on November 28th., it is possible the sarcophagus itself was unfinished.

The Westminster funeral was likely to have been the more public and prestigious and it was probably for this ceremony that Edward had called together 'the ruling nobility, pontiffs and prelates' (Walsingham and St. Alban's Chronicle). It is possible all the important guests had not arrived, although Oliver Sutton, who was to conduct this funeral probably accompanied the Cortège.

St. Alban's to Ermine Street

Though remnants of the Roman/Medieval road from St. Alban's to Ermine Street have survived, it is not possible to follow it by car, and difficult on foot. It may be traced using the O/S map Landranger series, sheet number 166.

The St. Alban's Cross site indicates the Cortège exit route, through the market, via St. Peter's Street, past the Church of St. Peter.

St. Peter's

Like St. Michael's, where the Convent had met the Cortège, St. Peter's had been a Saxon church founded by Abbot Ulsinus. It was largely re-built in the 13th. century, so was likely to have been new or even unfinished when the Cortège passed. It was re-built again in the 15th. century, but fragments of medieval glass may be seen on the North wall.

St. Peter's Street runs into Sandridge Road, the B651 to Sandridge. Just after Sandridge, the old road diverges from the B651 to die out after crossing the River Lea. It would have continued to the Domesday settlement of Welwyn, where it crossed the River Mimram. It is found again as the B197 to Oaklands, then, as a minor road and track, running to Walton-at-Stone, where it disappears to re-emerge near Sacombe. After being lost again across Labden's Farm, it joins Ermine Street just over 3 miles North of Ware - the total distance being c. 12½ miles.

Ermine Street to Waltham Abbey

   Ermine Street approximates to the A10 as far as Ware, after which road and drainage development have caused some alteration.   It continued to Waltham-on-the-Street, now, since the building of Eleanor's memorial, Waltham Cross. Here the River Lea had to be crossed, in order to reach the Abbey.   This River has now been transformed into a series of reservoirs, which have drained the surrounding land. Maps by Saxton (1579) and Blaeu (1662) show the River running in three channels between Waltham Cross and Waltham Abbey, each spanned by a separate bridge.   After crossing the River, the Cortège would have arrived at Waltham Abbey.

PART IX

Waltham

The Church of the Holy Cross at Waltham

The history of the early church at Waltham is given in 'De Inventione Santae Crucis Nostrae' written by one of the secular canons expelled from the Abbey in 1177. Therein it is claimed the first church had been established by Tovi the Proud, Cnut's standard bearer. After Cnut became King of England in 1017, he rewarded Tovi with the manor of Reading and property in Somerset. A cross, believed to possess miraculous properties, discovered on a Somerset estate, was brought to Waltham and housed in a parish church, which may have been purpose-built as it became known as the Church of the Holy Cross.

The Abbey

About 1058, Harold Godwinson, who was to become King of England in 1065, rebuilt the Church at Waltham 'from its foundations' and established a College of Secular Canons for the pastoral care of the villagers. These thirteen canons, who were allowed to own property and to marry, would have lived with their own families in the village. Harold's cruciform Church covered the present church together with an area marked out in the churchyard.

The Burial of Harold

Orderic claims that after his death at the Battle of Hastings Harold's body was buried on the beach: Malmesbury that it was given to his mother (Gytha) without ransome and interred at Waltham. The author of 'De Inventione' tells how two canons of Waltham obtained permission from Duke William of Normandy, in exchange for 10 marks of gold, to take the body of their benefactor. Being unable to identify Harold amongst the dead, they sent for Harold's mistress, Edith Swan-neck, who 'by his features' recognised him. The corpse was then interred in the Church at Waltham with 'regal honours'. Harold's mother fled to Flanders in 1067 (Anglo-Saxon Chronicle).

The destruction of the chancel of the Church at the Dissolution left Harold's grave outside and East of the surviving structure, where it may still be seen (*fig.1*). In the 17th. century Defoe had found:-

'no monument - only a grave stone on which was engraven 'Harold Infaelix' (Harold the Unhappy).'

1. Waltham Abbey Church showing 'Harold's Grave'

The Regular Canons

There was opposition to Secular Canons within the Catholic Church. In 1075 Pope Gregory VII ordered the laity to accept no further ministrations from married priests whom he deprived of their revenues.

At Waltham, the Secular Canons continued to minister to the parish for over another 100 years but during that time the opposition was increasing. A commune of celibate clergy known as Regular Canons, was established at Colchester by 1107. Under the patronage of Henry I and his Queen Edith/Matilda the Order spread and eventually celibacy became a condition for priesthood in the English Church. Inevitably, it was resisted and Bishop Grosseteste was still fighting to eliminate married clergy during his episcopate (1209-1235).

Henry II establishes the Priory

After his escape from Northampton Becket remained abroad for six years. In 1170 he was officially reconciled to

Henry II and returned to England. Twenty-six days later he was murdered before the altar at Canterbury, by four of Henry's household knights, possibly on the King's orders. In 1173 there was wide-spread revolt against Henry. Vengeance for Becket's death was given as one of the causes. The King defeated his enemies after doing public penance at Becket's tomb.

In further expiation he replaced the Secular Canons at Waltham with 26 Regular Canons and so a Priory was established. Henry expanded the Church to virtually triple its size, destroying its apsidal end, extending the building eastwards to include a second set of transepts and tower, and a new choir. Excavations carried out in 1955/6 and in 1984 have revealed the ground plan of Henry II's church.

The Priory becomes an Abbey

There was only one Prior. In 1184 the Priory was raised to Abbey status. The Abbot in 1290 was Robert de Elenton (1289-1302). At the Dissolution the Norman nave and its adjoining tower were accounted the parish church and survived the destruction which swept Henry II's buildings away.

2. Waltham Cross with the Falcon Inn, the Four Swans and the Victorian Railings after the 1889 Restoration

A late 13th. century Abbot's grave slab, recovered from the demolished part of the Church, may be seen in the present Church, together with a 13th. century coffin lid, near the monument to Captain Robert Smith. The brass was removed by a late 17th. century 'collector'.

In 1552 the tower fell. Material from its ruins were used to build a new tower, situated at the West end in order to buttress the Church which was leaning westwards. Further damage occurred during the 1939 War when blast from a land mine destroyed glass in the North aisle. The land-mine crater has been preserved.

The Cross at Waltham

After spending the night of December 13th. at Waltham Abbey, the Cortège re-crossed the River Lea to Ermine Street, and here, either on arrival or departure, selected the cross site, at the meeting of the two roads.

The Building of the Cross - craftsmen and costs

In the accounts, the first payment for the cross at Waltham was made in Autumn 1290, to Dymenge de Reynes (later also called de Leger) and Roger Crundale. It was a part payment of £10, the whole sum for the work being later defined as £95. After Easter 1291 Dymenge alone is named in these payments. Two shillings in excess of the £95 was given to Dymenge with Alexander the Image-maker. The final payment for work on the Cross was made in the Autumn of 1291. After this Dymenge and Alexander transferred to work on the Queen's tomb at Lincoln.

Caen stone for this cross was supplied/transported by Richard Crundale and Henry Mauger, one load being brought from London. 32 Caen stones were bought from Henry Mauger specifically for the Queen's images on Waltham and Charing crosses. As there were 6 images on the Cross at Waltham and, reputedly, 8 on Charing Cross, provided the stones were cut to a standard size, it would appear the images at Charing were not the same size as those at Waltham. 32 stones would share amongst the 14 images if 2 stones per image were allocated to Waltham, giving a total of 12 stones, and 2½ stones per image at Charing accounting for the remaining 20 stones, the larger images being in keeping with the larger (octagonal) cross.

The £10 given for these stones was recorded as a part payment, so that, even assuming the 12:20 allotment of the image stones to be correct, and dividing the £10 accordingly (£3.15s : £6. 5s.) the total cost of the stone for the Waltham Cross cannot be accurately assessed. The total payments of

£16 plus the controversial £3. 15s. would give a minimum cost of £19. 15s.

Robert de Corf was made 2 payments totalling 12 marks (£8) for 3 (sets of ?) rings, rods and hoods for the 3 crosses of Northampton, Lincoln and Waltham, shared equally amongst the 3 crosses this would give 4 marks each (£2.13s. 4d) making a total minimum cost for the Cross at Waltham of £117. 10s. 4d. (£95 + 2s + £19. 15s + £2.13s. 4d).

Damage and Restorations

Waltham Cross had originally been outside the village. There may have been a leper hospital and chapel nearby during the Middle Ages. This Cross survived the religious upheavals of the 16th. and 17th. centuries, but, by the 18th. century, was suffering damage from nearby building and increased traffic. Stukeley, in the 1728 letter to the Earl of Oxford concerning the Eleanor crosses is quoted as having written:-

'Waltham is pretty perfect, but, this last summer, Mrs. Robinson has re-built part of her house and encroached upon the road and broke down a good deal of the Cross to make way for her roof'.

Having referred to an inn near the Cross called 'The Four Swans' which 'bore the marks of great antiquity' Gough adds:-

'but the resort of travellers rendering another inn upon the spot necessary, the Cross, as now seen, (1796) has almost been taken into the end of it, whereby much of its beauty is concealed and many of its ornaments disfigured'.

Lysons, in 1796, names the inn adjoining the Cross as the 'Falcon'. (The Environs of London Vol IV). This inn, is shown, identified by the sign, in an engraving in Rimmer's 'Ancient Stone Crosses of England' (1875). On January 12th. 1889, a newspaper, commenting on the restoration of the Cross which had just been concluded reported:-

'Among the original pieces of carved stone which are now in the Cross are several pieces which for years had been buried in the walls of a local hotel'. The hotel is not identified but may have been the 'Falcon'. (*see fig.2*).

An engraving of Waltham Cross made by S. Harris, dated 1718 (Abel) shows the steps broken away. Stukeley (Letters and Diaries) wrote:-
'Waltham Cross was in much danger of being quite pulled down by carriages running against it. About the year 1720 I caused 2 oaken posts to be set down to keep off the

carriages'. In 1757, Lord Monson, at the Society of Antiquaries' request, 'surrounded the base with brickwork. By 1796 the Cross was reported much decayed. It was proposed to move it into 'the Park of the Theobalds' - a scheme which appears to have run over into the following century (Abel) but was eventually abandoned as the structure was considered too fragile.

3. Norman Arches Waltham Abbey Church

There were two major restorations during the 19th. century. The first in 1833/4 was under the direction of Mr. Bernard Clarke. The engraving in Rimmer shows the Cross after this restoration, with the head-cross but without the Victorian railings, erected before Abel's photograph (1864). The Bath stone used in this restoration was too soft, and a second renovation was deemed necessary in the 1880's. This brought to light the story of an old head cross, dug out of the foundations during Clarke's restoration. Believing this had headed the original structure, Clarke used it as a model for that cross with which he headed the renovated monument. On his death he had entrusted the original fragment to Mrs. Hall, an old retainer. It was produced during the 1880's restoration when it 'came into the hands of one of the Restoration Committee'. (Newspaper report - January 12th. 1889 published in 'A Swinethorpe and Harby Miscellany' Ed. Terence Leach).

The second 19th. century restoration was supervised by a Committee, finance being provided by public subscription. Promises of support were received from the Clothmakers' Company, Lord Aberdare, Lord Randolph Churchill (father of Winston) Sir T. Fowell Buxton, Sir John Lubbock, and 'about 30 Freemason Lodges'. Sir H.B Meux presented a piece of land valued at £2,000 for widening the roadway on one side of the Cross. Restoration work was carried out under C.E. Ponting F.S.A. diocescan surveyor for Wiltshire, aided by Harry Hemms 'the well-known sculptor'.

By this restoration, the Cross was left on an island at a junction between High Street and Eleanor Cross Road where it was particularly vulnerable to traffic. Between 1950 and 1953 further restoration was undertaken by Hertfordshire County Council. The original statues of the Queen were replaced by replicas commissioned from H. Thomas and Son of Chelsea and removed to Cheshunt Central Library. They are now in the Victoria and Albert Museum, London.

The 1989/90 Restoration
(A Report by Members of Hertfordshire County Council.)

The 1989 work was financed by Hertfordshire County Council, National Westminster Bank plc and English Heritage. A specialist Surveyor was commissioned to supervise the work, which was carried out by a specialist stone conservator.

The first requirement was the removal of years of accumulated pigeon droppings and general twentieth century dirt and debris to enable the detailed work to be specified, and the necessary approvals and consents obtained from English Heritage and the Department of the Environment.

The visible original Caen stonework was then carefully measured and photographed, and this record is retained with the archive of the repairs.

The fundamental principles of conservation were strictly adhered to during the whole of the work. No work was carried out unless it was necessary, and stonework was only replaced if required for the weathering of the monument, or because the piece being replaced was irreparably decayed or damaged.

The cleaning of the stonework involved hours of painstaking work, the layers of grime and carbon being softened by a controlled spray of clean water, in short bursts of a few minutes duration, interspersed with brushing the mouldings with small bristle brushes (toothbrush size). Where the removal of the carbon would have caused damage to the stone, it was left only partially clean.

The stonework of the more weathered areas and details is largely Victorian, which was carried out in Ketton stone. The original Caen stone, having eroded from those areas, was found in the protected niches, some areas at the bases of the pinnacles, and in the core of the monument behind the Ketton stone. Where a spall or lamination of the surface of the Caen stone had occurred, the space between the stones was sealed with a lime putty fillet after the removal of salts and frass from the cavity prior to grouting the void wherever possible. The extent of work to the several hundred finials and crockets was the subject of considerable debate with the eventual result that examples of each type of finial were replaced as a physical record, whilst the remainder of the demised stone was strengthened and protected with a thin layer of mortar made up from crushed stone dust, lime and silver sand with a thinner coat of the same mixture being used as a shelter coating on the areas just beginning to show signs of decay.

The lower gutter was carefully relined, and cavities filled in the upper, ensuring that water is now directed away from, rather than into, the monument. Replacement of decayed weathering of the parapets was also essential.

The whole of the stonework was then consolidated and protected with lime water, and a minimum amount of pigeon netting and wires fixed to reduce the damage caused by the pigeons which destroyed the coating of the monument.

To complete the work the Victorian railings were stripped of multiple layers of paint and repaired, prior to being refixed and painted. An archaeological excavation was organised to establish and record below ground details, prior to the final pedestrianisation of the area.

The Archaeological Dig

The excavations revealed that the steps from the Victorian restoration were some 15-18cms. below the existing level.

The original medieval foundations could be clearly seen alongside the footings of the once adjoining Falcon Hotel. From the excavation it would appear that the original curtilage of the Cross extended some 1.2 metres from its present boundary, possibly in the form of extra steps, which had been damaged or removed as the years passed.

The restored Waltham Cross may now be seen in the pedestrian precinct.

PART X

London

To London

From the Cross site, Ermine Street ran parallel to the River Lea, past Enfield, which Edward was to visit after Eleanor's Westminster funeral, and Tottenham, where the old cross has since been mistaken for one of Eleanor's memorials, down Stamford Hill and straight as Stoke Newington High Street and Road into Kingsland Road, where the present day equivalent, the A1010, becomes the A10. It would have passed the Hospital of St. Mary Spital and St. Botolph's Church, entering the City by Bishop Gate.

1. Edward Entering London

London Walls

London had been a Roman walled town with a square fort at the North-West corner. The walls on the North, West and East were renovated and still in use during the Middle Ages. Fitz-Stephen, writing between 1170 and 1182, claimed 'London once had its walls and tower....on the South, but that vast River, the Thames, has, in a long tract of time, totally subverted and carried away the walls in this part.'

The London Wall Walk

Other parts of the City wall have survived and may be seen by following the London Wall Walk, which is clearly sign-posted and labelled, but at present incomplete. From the Tower, travelling in an anti-clockwise direction, the 1290 City defences were probably as follows.

The Tower and Environs

A 12th. century extension took part of the Tower outside the wall, the old line of which ran through the present complex from Lanthom Tower to Bowyer Tower. Edward's Wardrobe (Treasury) at the Tower was raised on a bastion of the old Roman wall, part of which may be seen near St. John's Chapel. The Royal Wardrobe was removed in 1361.

The Tower Postern

Excavations in 1979 revealed a postern gate dated c. 1270, on the North side of the Tower, at the South end of what is now the Tower Hill Underpass. Built of Caen stone with a portcullis, this was a single gate. It has been suggested that it replaced a double gate but this is unlikely.

Fitz-Stephen claimed there were, in his time, seven double gates in the City wall, but he did not name them. Six of these are generally accepted as Aldgate, Bishopgate, Cripplegate, Aldersgate, Newgate and Ludgate. The seventh is considered to have been either Bridgegate, at London Bridge, or an earlier gate at the Tower. As an effective gate still existed across London Bridge in 1381, when it was closed against Wat Tyler (Froissart) this was more likely to have been the seventh of Fitz-Stephen's double gates.

St. Katherine's by the Tower

Just East of the Tower wall, outside the City, lay the Hospital of St. Katherine, founded by Henry I's wife, Edith/Matilda. It was revitalized by Eleanor. Stow (Survey of London) claims she established 3 regular canons and 3 sisters there to care for 10 poor women and 6 poor clerks.

In 1828 the surviving institution was moved to Regent's Park and the Church demolished to make way for St. Katherine's Docks.

The Tower to Aldgate

In this section two pieces of the Roman/Medieval wall have survived, and may be seen in a garden by the Northern entrance to the Tower Hill underpass, and, in a courtyard by the Bank Building (London Wall Walk).

Aldgate

Through this Roman gate lay the road to Colchester. The gate was in poor condition in 1215 when it allowed the barons in revolt against King John admittance to the City. It was repaired 'after the manner of the Normans, strongly arched, with bulwarks of stone from Caen in Normandy and small brick called Flanders tile', (Stow). Although a double gate in Fitz-Stephen's time, it was re-built with a single entrance. Completely restored in 1607-9, it was demolished in 1761. (*see fig. 2*).

2. Aldgate c.1759

The Priory of the Holy Trinity

From Aldgate to Bishopgate the line of the wall lay North-West, along Duke's Place. On this side of Aldgate stood the Priory of Holy Trinity. It had been founded by Queen Edith/Matilda on land belonging to Waltham Abbey. In compensation the Waltham Canons received a mill.

A group of citizens, called by Stow the Knight's Gild, gave the Priory an area of land with the soke, lying outside the City walls and stretching southwards to the River Thames, together with the Church of St. Botolph. This land became known as Port Soke, remembered in Portsoken Street. Having acquired and enclosed the passage between the Priory and the City wall, the Canons were able to make a gateway giving them direct access to this property outside. In 1977 a subway under Duke's Place cut through the City wall. Excavations revealed the Priory doorway, which had been blocked up in the 15th. century.

At the surrender of the Priory in 1531 it was given to Sir Thomas Audley, Speaker of the Parliament which had arraigned Wolsley, and who was later Henry VIII's Chancellor. Having demolished the 'great church' with some difficulty, Audley lived in the Priory buildings. After his death the property passed to his son-in-law, the Duke of Norfolk and the site became known as Duke's Place.

From Duke's Place the line of the wall continued North-West along Bevis Marks and Camomile Street to Bishop Gate.

Bishop Gate

Stow discovered a 1210 reference to this gate. At this, the Ermine Street entrance, a Roman gate would be expected. An inquest held in 1281 found that responsibility for its upkeep lay with the Hanseatic merchants based in London. These merchants rebuilt it in 1479, and were planning to do so again in 1551 when their assets were seized at the suit of the English merchants. Eventually the gate was rebuilt in 1735, only to be demolished 25 years later.

Bishop Gate to Cripples' Gate

This stretch, running on the North side of Wormwood Street and London Wall, constituted the North wall of the Medieval City. Outside lay farm land, idealized by Fitz-Stephen as 'cornfields, delightful meadows with pleasant streams on which stands many a mill.' Beyond was 'an immense forest.' By 1290, this forest had probably been reduced particularly by Henry III's demand for building timber, and the fields become more marshy with the neglect of the Town Ditch.

Moorgate

There are no indications of a double gate in 1290. Access to the fields must have been gained by one or more posterns. Moorgate, which emerges as the main gate in the North wall, may have originated as a postern. Stow gives a 1415 reference for this gate, saying it was 'made for the ease of the Citizens, that way to pass upon causeways into the field for their recreation.' The representation of this gate, shown on the 'Copper Plate Map' of c. 1553-1559 suggests an elaborate super-structure raised on a simple opening.

Cripples Gate

This gate, the northern entrance to the Roman fort, stood at the corner of Wood Street and St. Alphege Gardens. Stow gives several Saxon and Norman references for Cripplesgate and claims it was re-built by the Brewers in 1244. Their hall stands nearby.

The gate gave access to the moors and the vill of Islington. It also served as a prison. In 1285, Edward, after a disagreement with the Citizens of London, deposed the Mayor and appointed Ralph de Sandwich as City Warden and Tower Constable. Edward sent Ralph a writ ordering him to commit 'those guilty of debt and trespass to our prison of Criples Gate.'

Cripples Gate was defended by a barbican, given to the Earl of Suffolk in 1336. This area has been developed as The Barbican and includes The Museum of London. It has been suggested the gate was originally named because of an underground passage connecting it with the Barbican, through which it was necessary to creep - 'creep' and 'cripple' having similar origins.

Whatever the initial reasons for its name, the gate did become associated with beggars and cripples, and a church dedicated to St. Giles, their patron, was built outside by Alfune c. 1090.

The North wall of the Roman Fort was absorbed into the medieval City wall. Parts on both sides of Cripplegate have survived. The eastern section may be seen in St. Gile's Precinct and the western in St. Alphege Gardens.

Aldersgate

The West gate of the Roman Fort had been blocked (excavated 1959). A new gate at Aldersgate was probably built during the 4th. century.

An important gate, giving access to Smithfield, with its markets, fairs and sports facilities, and to the priory and hospital of St. Bartholomew, it served the Guildhall area - the 'Alderman's Bury' and was destroyed in 1760.

Outside Aldersgate

In 1257 the Friars of the Sack were established 'just

outside Aldersgate'. Being given the Jewish synagogue in 1271, they moved to Coleman Street, near the present Fenchurch Street Station, but then a market area. Here they complained that 'the howling of the Jews next door' disturbed their devotions. To-day Crutched Friars runs into Jewry Street.

The Priory of St. Bartholomew

Rahere, aided by Alfune, the architect of St. Giles, Cripplesgate, and Hagno the Clerk, built a priory and hospital dedicated to St. Bartholomew, on a tract of marsh outside Aldersgate, known as Smoothfield, (Smithfield). It was claimed by Thomas of Canterbury that 'Henry I granted the site in frankalmoign (free of Knight's service) and by his charter (1133) confirmed it.'

The Priory was initially for 13 regular canons. Rahere was its first Prior and Master of the hospital. One of the canons wrote 'the Book of the Foundation of the Church of St. Bartholomew' which is preserved in the British Museum. (Cott. Vesp BIX).

St. Bartholomew's Hospital

Though nothing of Rahere's hospital, or of the later 12th. century hospital chapel, remains above ground, the present hospital, designed by Gibbs, stands on the same site. The Chapel is largely 19th. century. Alms of 6s. 8d. were paid to this hospital by Queen Eleanor's executors. (Accounts, Autumn 1291).

Newgate

The London Wall Walk finishes at Aldersgate, but the wall to the River Thames continued by way of Newgate. Stow gave a 1218 order for this gate, which was then being used as a jail, as it was in 1290. In the accounts of the Queen's executors the Prison of Newgate received 20 shillings on the morrow of the anniversary of her death (November 29th. 1291).

Stow claims this gate was built as an alternative West exit to Ludgate, as the old East-west City way from Aldgate to Ludgate had been 'stopped up' by the extension of the walled precincts of St. Paul's. This would place Newgate after 1084. However, in 'Archaeologia' Vol. LIX, some evidence is given by Dr. Philip Norman for a Roman Gate at this point.

Newgate was repaired by Richard Whittington in 1422. In the 17th. century, images from this gate were used to decorate Newgate prison.

Just inside Newgate, the Franciscans established the first Friary in the City (1224).

Ludgate

The wall continued Southwards from Newgate to Ludgate. This was probably the Roman West gate. It is claimed it took its name from the legendary King Lud, who also inspired the Roman name of Londinium.

Stow tells how this gate was repaired in 1216, probably with stone from the Jewish houses which had been destroyed by the rebel barons in 1216. When the gate was repaired again in 1260, a licence was granted to the Citizens for stone to make images of Lud and other kings with which to decorate the gate. The 1586 re-build, which uncovered stone inscribed with Hebrew characters, included images of Lud and his two sons on the East and one of Queen Elizabeth I on the West. When the gate was destroyed in 1760 these images were preserved and may now be seen in the vestry porch of St. Dunstan in the West. It is possible these are the only surviving remnants of any city gate and that this representation of Queen Elizabeth I is the oldest in stone.

St. Paul's Monastery

Edith Bradley's map shows how Ludgate was blocked by St. Paul's. A Saxon church here, reputedly founded by Ethelbert, of Kent in the 7th. century, was destroyed by fire; another by Vikings in 962 and a third by fire in 1087. The fourth church on the site, started by Maurice, Bishop of London, under William II, was dedicated in 1240. Eighteen years later a programme of extension and re-building was initiated which was still in progress in 1290. The church was extended eastwards to a length of 596 feet, destroying the parish church of St. Faith in the process The Norman nave was replaced by one in the fashionable Gothic style and the spire eventually (1316) raised to 489 feet. Extensive walled precincts with six gates were established around the Cathedral.

This area was given over to housing and shops after the Reformation but the church survived, probably because the parishioners of St. Faith's had been allowed to use part of the crypt as their parish church. (*see fig. 3*).

The church was deprived of its assets, severely damaged by fire, and gradually decayed. 17th. century re-building was stopped when, during the Civil War, Parliament appropriated the repair fund and scaffolding to pay their troops. Plans for repair were under consideration when Old St. Paul's was so badly damaged in the Great Fire of London that a complete re-build became necessary and Wren's church, the present church and the fifth on the site, came into being.

3. The East End of Old St. Paul's showing St. Faith's Crypt

The 13th. century Wall Extension

From Ludgate to the River Thames the old wall, in 1290, was being extended to the Fleet River in order to accommodate the new Dominican Friary. In 1282 Edward had granted a licence to break and take down the wall and allotted the custom or toll (taxes) of the City to rebuild it from Ludgate, West, to Fleet Bridge (Ludgate Circus), behind the houses along the water of the Fleet to the River Thames. This realignment is shown on Stow's and on Hogenburg's maps of London. The course of the Fleet River, now culverted, approximates to Farringdon Street and New Bridge Street, entering the Thames about Blackfriars Bridge. The wall rebuilding appears to have been prolonged into the reign of Edward II when the citizens of London were commanded to 'make up' the wall and tower at the end. (Rolls 1310).

The New Dominican Friary

The London Black Friars had originally been established in Holborn, probably in Shoe Lane. This house had been sold. Land for a new Friary near the Thames had been in the hands of Robert Kilwarby, the Dominican Archbishop of Canterbury, since 1276, when he had been granted the site and tower of Montfichet and two lanes 'next the street of Baynard's Castle.'

Monfichet and Baynards, Fitz-Stephen's two well fortified castles 'on the West' were named after the Conqueror's barons who founded them on the River Thames. Both had been slighted in 1213 and their owners, Robert Montfichet and Robert Fitzwater, to whom Baynards had passed via the Clares, were banished. Montfichet was to be replaced by the new Dominican Friary, but Baynards was restored when Robert Fitzwater regained King John's favour, and was likely to have been standing in 1290. It was rebuilt by Humphrey, Duke of Gloucester after 1428.

The New Friary, established in the area which is still known as Blackfriars, was to be a prestigious foundation. Stow reports the church was large and richly furnished, the Friary was the venue of many parliaments and that Eleanor and Edward were great benefactors. A list of monumental tombs there includes those of Hubert de Burgh, Justician and Earl of Kent, brought from the Holborn monastery, and members of the Arundel, Clare, Valence, and Beauchamp families. There, also, had been buried the heart of Edward and Eleanor's third son Alfonse, who had died in 1284. Eleanor's own heart burial at Black Friars is likely to have taken place on December 15th.

Heart Burials

The separate burial of a heart was fairly common during the Middle Ages, and not unknown in this century. The most famous was probably that of Robert the Bruce, King of

Scotland (died 1329), whose heart, encased in silver was being carried by Douglas to the Church of the Holy Sepulchre at Jerusalem, when Douglas was killed in battle. The burial eventually took place at Melrose Abbey.

Separate heart burials provided a solution for those divided in allegiance either to places or people. In 1928 Thomas Hardy's body was buried in Westminster Abbey, but his heart in his first wife's grave. (Encyclopaedia Britannica).

The Queen's Heart Chapel and Tomb

Although £100 had been paid for the Queen's heart tomb on February 18th. 1290, a further payment was made to Robert of Newmarket in the Spring of 1291 for pavement and other necessities (£4. 17s. 9d). A Master William the Artist, who may also have been William de Dunolmia (Durham?) was paid for painting about the Queen's tomb 'without lettering'. A Walter de Dunolmia, if also Walter the Artist, received a total of £6. 5s. 8d. for the same task. By the spring of 1292 Walter Dunolmia was working on the paintings around the tomb at Westminster.

William de Hoo, identified as cementario, worked on a crest, above the tomb, probably carved from stone, for which he was paid £1. 13s. 4d. Master Robert Colebroke was mentioned in connection with a hearse, (see under Westminster). A cloth was painted to hang above the 'Queen's heart'.

Although Heart Tombs were usually small, the amount of wax and metal ordered for the Black Friars image suggests there was a full size effigy and tomb. (see under 'Westminster'). £7. 13s. 4d. was paid to Alexander the Imagemaker and Dymenge de Leger for wax for 3 small images, cast of 'appropriate metal' by William de Suffolk of London, for this and the Lincoln tomb. William Torel, responsible for the large image at Westminster and possibly that at Lincoln, is not associated with that at the Dominican Friary, London in the executor's accounts.

The Fate of the Friary

In 1546, near the end of Henry VIII's reign, the Friary was granted to Sir Thomas Cheney. Under two years later it came to Sir Francis Bryan and in 1549/50 to Sir Thomas Carden, by whom, according to Stow it was demolished. The parish church of St. Anne had lain within the Friary precincts and Queen Mary forced Sir Thomas to re-habilitate its parishioners, which he did by providing 'a chamber above a stair.' When this collapsed, a new church dedicated to St. Anne was built (1597). It was destroyed in the Great Fire of 1666, but a fragment of the Friary survived above ground, in the corner of the churchyard.

Archaeologists, currently working around the River Fleet, have discovered stones from the Friary beneath the arches of a Victorian viaduct and remains of the 13th. century city wall under Pilgrim Street.

London's Churches

Fitz-Stephen claimed there were 125 parish churches in London and the suburbs. Four hundred years later, Stow recorded 96 parish churches inside the medieval walls, including St. Mary Axe and St. Augustine in the wall which had, by then, been suppressed.

The Great Fire damaged most of the medieval city churches - the Victoria County History claims 89 out of 97. To-day there are probably 30 churches within the limits of the old medieval city which bear the same dedications and occupy the sites of their 13th. century fore-runners. Twenty of these had been re-built by Wren or Hawksmore, some only to be damaged or destroyed in the 20th. century wars. Several are no longer used as churches. Some have double dedications recalling more than one early church.

Thirteen large conventual churches were claimed by Fitz-Stephen for London and the suburbs. Inevitably most churches or parts of churches used by the convents were destroyed at the Dissolution, a notable exception being that of St. Helen's. Pevsner describes the 'fragment of a Benedictine nunnery with the nuns' church completely preserved' as 'an unexpected relic, hidden behind the massive office buildings of Bishopsgate.'

This church was dedicated to St. Helen, mother of the Emperor Constantine and founder of the Church of the Holy Sepulchre at Jerusalem. It came into the possession of St. Paul's. In 1210 William Basing, the Dean, established a priory of Black nuns in the churchyard. The Priory church was built on the west side of the parish church and the parish church nave was extended to join it, creating an unusual double nave. Although the conventual buildings were destroyed, the Youngs (London's Churches) note 'an odd little staircase in the North wall which originally led to the nuns' dormitory'. They also claim 'Edward I presented a piece of the 'True Cross' which he had found in Wales' to the church, in 1285.

This may have been of the cross he and Eleanor processed to Westminster in that year.

More detailed information on London's churches may be found in London Volume 1 in the Buildings of England series by Pevsner. A Guide to London's Churches by Mervyn Blatch (Constable) and London's Churches by Elizabeth and Wayland Young (Grafton).

Trade and Commerce

The central market area of the City is recalled in Poultry, Cornhill, and Cheapside, ceap being Old English for 'to barter'. By the 13th. century, the North bank of the River Thames had been extended and developed to accommodate docks and wharves (gates) such as Billingsgate, mentioned by Geoffrey of Monmouth, and Queenhythe, the property of Edward's mother. Fitz-Stephen records wine sold from ships and vaults on the River bank, and a remarkable public eating house and 'take-away'. This offered a wide choice of food and was 'open all hours'.

It was in the market area, in Cheapside at the end of Wood Street, Elearnor's eleventh memorial cross was erected.

The Cheapside Cross

In the Executors' Accounts payments for Cheap cross were made to one man only, Master Michael of Cantuaria (Canterbury?) cimentario. The contract price is given as £300 (Michaelmas Term 1292) but the total of the ten payments recorded amounts to £226. 13s. 4d. The first payment of £50 was made at the end of the Michaelmas Term 1290 (early in 1291 by our reckoning), and the last in the Michaelmas Term 1292, by which time the Cross had moved into its 'operations' stage. Three hundred pounds was not necessarily the total cost of this cross, which may have been supplied with some of the undirected images, rods, rings and hoods and materials.

The Appearance of Cheap Cross

No structural detail can be deduced from the Executors' Accounts, which merely record the payments for 'work' and 'operations'. Known pictorial representation of this cross have been made after it was re-built during the 15th. century.

Walter of Guisborough wrote 'In her memory the King himself erected two most beautiful crosses of marble, one in Charing, and the other in West Cheap.' Two surviving fragments of Cheap Cross, recovered during the reconstruction of a Cheapside sewer and preserved in The Museum of London, are of marble. They bear the shields of England and Castile quartered Leon, with which this Cross must have been decorated. (*see fig. 4*).

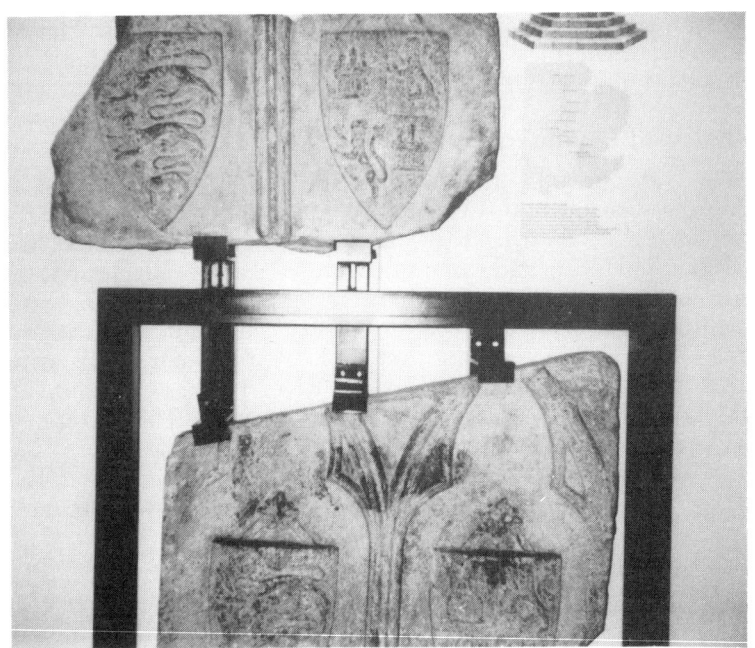

4. Fragments from the Cheapside Cross in the Museum of London

Fate

In 1441 the Cross being 'by length of time decayed' wrote Stow, John Hatherley (whom he gives as Mayor in the year 1431) Mayor of London, obtained a Licence from King Henry VI to 're-edify the same in a more beautiful manner'. The Cross was 'then' (1484-1486) 'curiously wrought at the charges of divers citizens'. Stow saw this renovated cross in situ and his references to the lower images around the monument of Christ's resurrection, the Virgin Mary with the Christ child in her arms stayed on her knees, and St. Edward the Confessor, suggest the Cross had been re-made, with a stronger religious emphasis, rather than restored.

During the late 16th. and the 17th. centuries this cross attracted much resentment. It was seen as a traffic hazard by certain members of the public, who, by 'divers inquests' sought to have it removed. The timber cross encased with lead, by which this monument was surmounted, had rotted, and was 'feared to have fallen to the harm of some people below'. Stow reported that in 1581, 1599 and 1600 the cross images had been defaced.

It had been the custom to gild the Cross for certain royal occasions, one having been the arrival of Philip of

Spain in 1554. The Catholic and Royalist associations rendered this cross abhorrent to the Parliamentarian iconoclasts. Personified as Antichrist, it became a focus of their hatred and was pulled down by the London citizens with the permission of Parliament. The mayor and alderman watched while 'antichrist' was thrown into the flames. The bells of St. Peter's rang a merry peal, the city waits played melodious tunes on the leads of the church, the train bends discharged volleys of musquetry and the spectators celebrated the triumph with acclamations of joy'. (*see fig. 5*).

5. The Destruction of Cheapside Cross

The Journey Through London

Edward signed writs in London on December 14th. and 15th. indicating the Cortège arrived on the 14th. and stayed in London for at least that night. While there, the Queen's heart burial took place, the cross site was selected and the Priory of the Holy Trinity was visited.

Bishop Gate, as the bar on Ermine Street, was its most likely way of entrance, but Aldgate cannot be totally dismissed. There was probably a way connecting Ermine Street and the Colchester Road running outside the city wall. The Priory of the Holy Trinity was nearer Aldgate. If the Court wished to honour the custom of giving thanks to St. Bartholomew for a safe journey, both gates were provided with a church dedicated to this Saint.

The Cortège stops at the Priory of the Holy Trinity

On February 20th. 1291 the canons and Prior at Holy Trinity were released from a fine of £100 and £10 in respect of that fine 'for the honour they did to the body of the Queen when she passed through'. 'Passed through' indicates the Cortège did not spend the night there. After stopping, it must have continued by the City's main East-West thoroughfare, Cornhill and Poultry to Cheapside, where the Cross site was selected, and where the Queen's bier may have been set down. Froissart recorded that Richard II's body lay in Cheapside 'the space of two hours' and was viewed by more than 20,000 persons.

Cheapside was blocked by the Church and walled grounds of the Austin canons of St. Paul's. In order to reach the Dominican Friary it would have been necessary to skirt or pass through the grounds. No reference to a St. Paul's stop has emerged, but by this time the day must have been advanced and the Cortège anxious to conclude the day's business.

The time factor would suggest that the heart burial at the Black Friary took place the following day, December 15th., after a vigil had been kept on the night of the 14th. No more writs are signed from that of December 15th. until after the final funeral, so it is not certain whether the Cortège left the Dominicans on the 15th. after the heart burial, or on the following day, when they were likely to have brought the Queen to Westminster Abbey in preparation for her final burial on Sunday December 17th.

PART XI
London to Westminster

To Charing (Cross)

1. London - showing Ludgate, the Black Friary and church Old St. Paul's and the Tower

For the Cortège to reach Westminster it was necessary to cross the Fleet River. Stow records a timber bridge between the Dominican Friary and the 'House of Bridewell' (shown on Edith Bradley's map), but, in 1290, the palace built upon that site was in ruins and this bridge could have been out of commission. A more appropriate way for the Cortège to leave the City would have been by Ludgate, crossing the Fleet by the main bridge. (*see fig. 1*).

The road from Ludgate to Charing had probably altered little since 1247, when Henry III had carried the 'blood of Christ' from St. Paul's to Westminster Abbey by way of the Bishop of Durham's palace (Matthew Paris). In 1442, when this highroad was 'very ruinous' (Stow), it had run 'before and nigh the manor of Savoy'. In the 13th. century this part of the route was known as the Strand, then the shore of the Thames.

To-day's equivalent is to 'cross the Fleet' by Ludgate Circus and come to Charing Cross by way of Fleet Street and the Strand. The latter has now been divided from the Thames by the Victoria Embankment, built on land taken from a narrower and deepened river.

The first part of this route is covered by Edith Bradley's 'London about 1300' (*see fig. 2*). Bath Palace and the Somerset House Complex are not covered. The Savoy Palace to Westminster Abbey can be followed on the map of Ralph Aggas (*see fig. 3 and page vi*).

Fleet Street

On the North side there was little development in 1290. Trackways led to Holborn, a settlement on the Old Bourne, a tributary of the Fleet River. In New Street, now Chancery Lane, Henry III had established a house for converted Jews (1246 Lib. Rolls). In 1290 a Walter de Amondesham was master there.

Immediately after the Fleet Bridge (Ludgate Circus) on the South side lay the ruins of St. Bride's, a palace used by Edward's father, Henry III. Stow claimed the Eastern part of this site remained as waste until Henry VIII built Bridewell Palace there, in 1553 to become a 'house of correction for vagabonds and loose women'. This building was demolished in 1863.

St. Bridget or Bride of Kildare died in 523. The early church dedicated to her in this place, was near a well, and so the district became known as Brideswell. The present Wren church, built 1678 was gutted in 1940, restored, and re-dedicated in 1957.

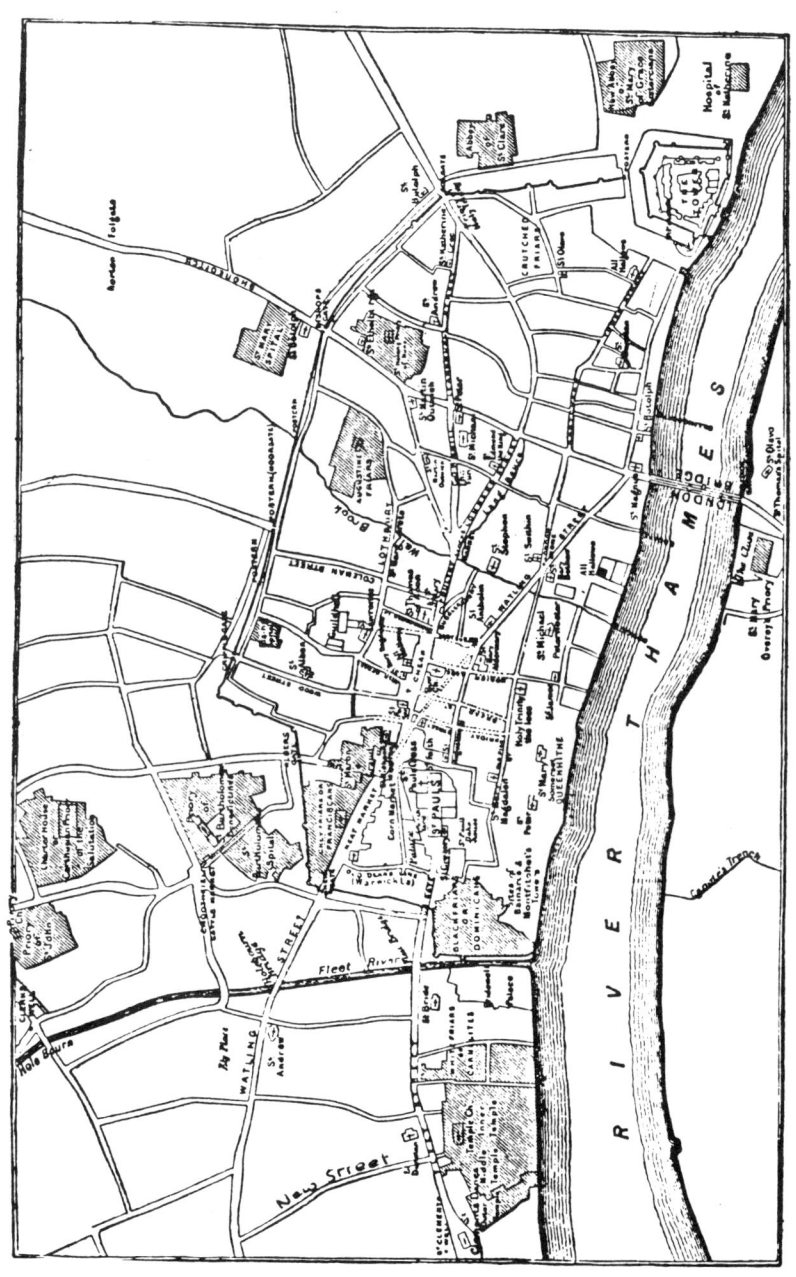

2. London c.1300
by Edith Bradley

The Carmelite Friary

Next to the ruined palace stood the Carmelite Friary. This had been founded in 1241 by Sir Richard Grey (V.C.H.) The site is recalled in Whitefriars Street and Carmelite Street. 1290 had been a bad year for the friars, many of whom had died, due, it was claimed, to 'filth in the lane' adjoining. The political activity of the White Friars increased after the suppression of their powerful neighbours, the Knights Templars.

The Temple

The Knights Templars had moved to this site from Holborn in 1161. Their new property on the River covered the area now known as the Inner and Middle Temple, and, in addition the Outer Temple, stretching from Middle Temple Lane to Essex Street, thus moving into the present Strand.

The Templars' Church

Their new church, situated in the Inner Temple section, was dedicated in 1185 by Heraclius, the Patriarch of Jerusalem. Like the Jerusalem church of St. Helen and Holy Sepulchre at Northampton, it was a 'round' church, another of the 4/5 to have survived in England. In keeping with contemporary taste, a rectangular choir was added in 1240, the dedication taking place in the presence of King Henry III.

The new Temple became a depository for valuables. It had been used by Hubert de Burgh, the Justiciar. On his fall in 1232 the Templars refused to release his property without his consent. Edward's mother, Eleanor of Provence, kept her jewels there. Edward had used this as a pretext to gain admission to the building in 1283. He removed £1,000 worth of valuables from the Templars' treasury. A small room, discovered beneath the south aisle of the choir of this church, is believed to have been the Templars' strong room.

After the suppression of the Order, the Outer Temple came to the Bishops of Exeter, who had their London palace there. This site passed to Robert Dudley during Elizabeth's reign and then to his step-son, Essex, who built Essex House, re-called in Essex Street. The Middle and Inner Temples passed to the Knights Hospitallers, who, in 1343/4 let them to law students. At the Dissolution the lease passed to the Crown. The lawyers were allowed to purchase the property in the 17th. century.

The Temple church was restored by Wren and 19th. century architects. The rectangular choir roof, damaged by incendiary bombs in 1941, fell on the effigies of the knights below. The purbeck marble pillars split in the heat.

The church was restored and re-dedicated in the presence of the Queen Mother in 1954.

The Effigies

Stow counted 11 effigies in the West ambulatory of this church. 8 being of armed knights, 5 with their legs crossed and 3 straight legged. He identified four of the images as those of William Marshal, who had fought against the supporters of Louis of France at 'The Fair of Lincoln' (died 1219), William Marshal the Younger, his son (died 1231), Gilbert Marshal, who was killed during a tournament at Hertford in 1241, and Robert Rose, who joined the Templars in 1245.

Nine effigies may now be seen. They have been repaired and moved so that they no longer indicate the site of burial. In a recess on the south aisle is a 13th. effigy of an unknown bishop, fully robed, with a dragon (the symbol of evil) at his feet.

Fleet Street was widened between Ludgate Circus and Temple Bar 1897-1916.

The Strand - St. Clement's Danes

On the Strand, opposite the Outer Temple stood a church dedicated to St. Clement. This saint, having been sent to the Crimea, was cast into the sea, with an anchor round his neck and drowned, during an early Roman persecution of the Christians. Consequently, though hardly propitiously, he was adopted by sailors as their patron saint.

At an early date this church became known as St. Clement's Danes. Several theories have been offered to explain the Danish connection. Stow's story of the reburial at this church of the body of Cnut's son, Harold, after it had been exhumed and cast out by his brother, Hardicnut, suggests a pre-Conquest church on this site. One existed in 1189, when the advowson was in the hands of the Templars.

The Wren Pierce rebuild was badly damaged in 1941. In 1955 the sailors' church was restored as a church for the allied and Commonwealth air-forces. It now stands on an island in the Strand. (End of 'London c.1300')

The Bishops' Palaces

Bishops and Archbishops with their household clerks had long been drawn into the secular service of the Kings. The establishment of Bishops' palaces or inns between London and Westminster during the 13th. century indicates the growth of the latter as an administrative centre. The Bishop of Ely's palace had been in Holborn but others, like the 14th. century Exeter Palace on the Outer Temple site, were established along the strand of the River Thames.

Bath Palace

The Bishop of Bath's palace stood next to the Outer Temple. The date of the first building here is not known but it would seem appropriate that Robert Burnell, Edward's Chancellor and Bishop of Bath, should have a London residence. A later palace was 'newly built' by Lord Thomas Seymour, Lord High Admiral and one of Henry VIII's many brothers in law. It came to the Earl of Arundel and was called Arundel House. The site is marked by Arundel Street.

The Somerset House Complex

According to Stow, Somerset, 'Protector' of the young Edward VI, demolished the Church of St. Mary-le-Strand, and the houses of the Bishops of Chester (Lichfield and Coventry) and Worcester to make way for his new house in the Strand. He was executed before the building was completed and the house became Crown property. The present Somerset House is late 18th. century with 19th. century additions.

The Bishop of Chester, Lichfield and Coventry's house or inn, if built by Edward's Treasurer, Walter Langton, as Stow suggests, may not have been standing in 1290. Walter became Treasurer in 1296 and Bishop in, or after, 1295.

Three Bishops of Worcester, prior to 1290, were involved at Court, and therefore could have established a bishop's house on the Strand. Walter Grey, a royal nominee, was Bishop for only one year, and Nicholas Ely for two, although he was Chancellor. Walter Cantilupe Bishop from 1237-1266 is the most likely candidate.

St. Mary-le-Strand

A church dedicated to St. Mary in the Strand was probably founded in 1130. It is claimed Thomas Becket was rector here before his rise to eminence. Its dedication was changed to the Church of the Nativity of Our Lady and the Innocents before its demolition.

Somerset was unable to fulfil his promise to provide the deprived parishioners with a new church. They worshipped at the Savoy chapel until the present church of St. Mary-le-Strand was built by Gibbs probably North of the earlier site.

This Savoy chapel, the property of the Queen, still stands, marking the site.

This church of St. Mary is, like St. Clement's Danes, on an island in the Strand. It is no longer used as a parish church, this parish having been amalgamated with that of St. Clement's.

Savoy House

In 1245 Henry III granted to his wife's uncle, Peter of Savoy 'all those houses on the Thames which sometime pertained to Brian de Insula or L'isle, in the way or street called the Strand'. Brian de L'isle had been a trusted servant to Henry's father, King John. He had been denounced by Henry in 1233 for being concerned in the death of the Earl Marshal, Richard of Pembroke, which had taken place in Ireland.

Peter of Savoy built a house on the site. On his death he left the property to the Hospice of St. Bernard in Savoy, but Queen Eleanor of Provence bought her uncle's house back for her younger son, Edmund, Earl of Lancaster, who re-built it. This was the house standing in 1290. (*See fig. 3 the Map of Ralph Aggas*).

The estate, together with the Earldom of Lancaster passed by marriage to John of Gaunt. The house was badly damaged in the Peasants' Revolt of 1381 (Froissart).

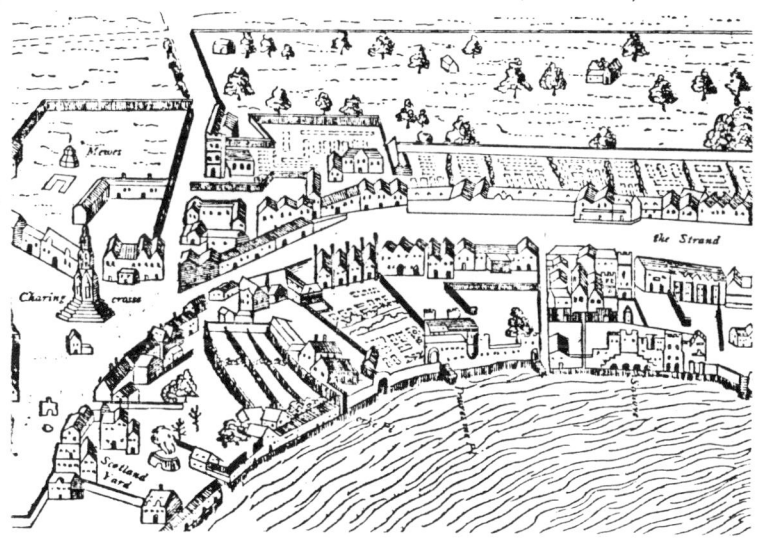

3. Ralph Aggas' Map

The Convent Garden

Opposite the Savoy Palace lay the convent garden, believed to have belonged to the monks of Westminster Abbey. At the West end of this was a church, known as St. Martin's in the fields.

There had been a church there in 1222, which may have been a chapel of ease for the monks working in the Convent's garden or fields. Another building was raised in 1544 which was declared a parish church. This is the church shown on the Aggas map. The present structure is basically the 18th. century church designed by Gibbs.

Durham Palace

Next to Savoy House stood the Durham House, which Stow claimed was founded by Anthony Bek, Bishop of Durham from 1284 to 1311. He was the son of a Lincolnshire baron, a close friend of Edward and Eleanor, who accompanied them on their crusade, and Patriarch of Jerusalem. Bek may have re-built the house during his term as Bishop, but, a Liberate Roll ordering repairs to the quay in 1239, and a mention of the gates of Durham House by Matthew Paris in 1247 indicate a house on the site prior to Bek. The initial building could have been the work of Richard Marsh, who had been Chancellor, and Bishop of Durham from 1217 to 1226 or of Richard le Poor, Bishop 1229 to 1237, though this was less likely since repairs were necessary in 1239.

According to Stow, the house was re-built by Bishop Hatfield (1545-1581). This may explain the different representations of this building given by Aggas and Antonie van den Wyngaerde (*see figs. 3 and 4*). The former would appear to be of the earlier house.

4. Durham House by Antonie van den Wyngaerde

Charing

This settlement between London and Westminster probably derived its name from the Saxon word 'cierre' (to turn) as it was situated at the bend in the River Thames. Another Charing, in Kent, was sited at a bend in the Pilgrim's Way.

There had been an anchorite at Charing. Henry III had provided a veil for his niece (Liberate Rolls). Unlike Hermits, anchorites were total prisoners, walled up or chained (i.e. anchored) in their cells, which indicates there had been a cell at Charing.

St. Mary Rouncivall

Apart from the Church of St. Martin's and the anchorite's cell the only other religious building in Charing appears to have been the convent of St. Mary Rouncivall. This had been founded by William Marshall the Elder (died 1219) who had been buried at the Temple. He gave several tenements (properties held by tenants) to the Prior of Rouncivall in Navarre for this convent. Stow says it was changed to a brotherhood and so survived the closure of alien houses in England. It was finally suppressed at the Reformation and the land used, again, for tenements.

In 1605, the Earl of Northampton, Henry Howard, built Northampton House on part of the site. This was acquired by the Duke of Northumberland, renamed Northumberland House, demolished in 1874 and Northumberland Avenue cut through the grounds. The site of St. Mary, Rouncivall has been placed between 'York Buildings and Northumberland House on the South side of the Strand', in which case it would have included the area now occupied by Charing Cross Station, and have stood, in 1290, next to Durham House.

Charing Cross

At Charing, afterwards known as Charing Cross, the last of Eleanor's twelve memorial crosses was raised.

The manufacture of this Cross raises certain questions. It appears to have taken longer to complete than any other cross, having been the first and last mentioned in the accounts, and to have cost more, yet the resultant monument does not seem to have been more impressive than the Northampton or Waltham crosses, which appear to be of the same type.

It has been suggested Charing Cross was expensive because of the amount of Corfe marble used in its manufacture. There is evidence that a large quantity of marble was used. In addition to Walter Guisborough's reference, the executors' accounts record payments for marble ashlars, suggesting the structure was marble faced, and also for marble steps. After this Cross was destroyed, Lilly, ('Observations On the Death of King Charles') wrote:-

'I have seen knife hafts made of some of the stones, which, being well polished, look like marble.' They probably were!

Payments specifically for marble, totalled £96. 12s. 1d. The Caen and unidentified stone, supplied by Henry Mauger and Ralph de Cycestria totalled £32. 3s. 5d. Other costs included the building of a workshop at Charing for the construction of the Cross, which was carried out by Robert de Colebroke and cost £3. 16s. 8d., carriage of stone and the cost of the images, likely to have been relatively small amounts. This leaves the wages bill as the most substantial single item.

The main craftsman, Master Richard Crundale, cimentarius, died between September 8th. and the middle of October 1292, before the cross was completed, but after it had entered the 'operations' stage. He was paid, including a post-mortem settlement, more than £549. 14s. 7d. for his work on this cross. It is impossible to be more precise, as some figures are missing due to document damage, one payment was a composite and the arrears were a part payment.

The work on the cross was finished by Robert Crundale - a relative, since the partial arrears were paid to him. He received a further £63. 17s. 10d. for his work, bringing the total labour costs to £613. 12s. 5d. - over six times the cost of the marble.

Accountancy Problems

The Crundales had to pay their work-force and it is possible, that, even the 13th. century, London wages were higher than those paid in the rest of the country. Nevertheless, a wages bill around four times the total cost of other crosses might cause a modern accountant to consider the possibility of fraud or careless book-keeping.

There is some evidence of the latter in the accounts. It is difficult to discover how the total given at the end of Michaelmas Term 1291 equates with the individual payments. There are instances throughout the accounts where the total part-payments exceed the original amount agreed. (When they fall below there is the possibility of this being remedied later). In spite of the counters with which the clerks were provided, roman numerals and mixed coinage (£.s.d. and marks) must have made addition a difficult task.

A Description of Charing Cross

The best known representation of this cross is the Crowle Collection drawing in the British Museum. Small sketches have survived e.g. in Wyngaerde's drawings of London and in the map of Ralph Aggas both drawn when the cross was still standing. As soon as these representations are compared differences appear. There are five steps in the Map and four in the Crowle drawing. (*see fig. 5*). Wyngaerde makes the structure taller, more slender and headed with a cross, whereas the other two are more squat and headless. Apart from the marble components, little in the accounts aids the cross's 'reconstruction'. Payments for the other stone finished by Easter 1292, which, with the evidence of the marble ashlars, suggests this was used for the core of the cross. Stone for paving and images of the Queen (see Waltham) is also mentioned. The latter were made by Alexander the Image-maker.

It is generally accepted this was an octagonal cross, bearing eight images of the Queen, elements which E.M. Barry incorporated into his substitute cross, now standing outside Charing Cross Station.

The Destruction of Charing Cross

Unlike the Cheapside Cross, that at Charing appears to have been tolerated and even regarded with some affection. After these crosses had been doomed by Parliament in 1643 there was not the same haste to remove it and it stood until 1647. The response to its demise, as shown by the verses in Percy's 'Reliqes' demonstrates wry regret, rather than fierce triumph.

> 'Undone, undone the lawyers are;
> They wander about the towne;
> Nor can find the way to Westminster
> Now Charing Cross is down.'

Lilley claimed some of the stones were used to pave 'before Whitehall' (palace), so some remnants may yet be recovered. The equestrian statue of King Charles I now stands on the cross site.

Charing to Westminster

The medieval way from Charing to Westminster Abbey and the King's palace, lay along King Street. This no longer exists. To-day's substitutes are Whitehall, Parliament Street, and the east side of Parliament Square.

5. Charing Cross - a reconstruction based on the drawing now in the Crowle collection at the British Museum

York Palace

The medieval house of the Archbishops of York stood on the Riverside, between St. Mary Rouncivall and the King's palace. The property had belonged, originally, to Hubert de Burgh, Earl of Kent, the Justician who fell from power in 1232. He gave it to the Black Friars of Holborn. They sold it to Walter Grey, Archbishop of York from 1215 to 1255, who used it as a palace from 1248.

Thomas (later Cardinal) Wolsey, Archbishop of York 1514-1530, enlarged and enhanced the property which at the Dissolution came into the hands of Henry VIII. A gallery, gate-houses (*see Aggas Map page vi*) and sports facilities were added and the house became known as the Palace of Whitehall. It was destroyed by fire in 1698, when only the Inigo Jones banqueting suite survived.

York Gate

York Water Gate, at present standing in Embankment Gardens, does not mark this first Archbishop of York's house, but the site of Suffolk House, given by Queen Mary Tudor to her Archbishop of York. (York Place on Aggas Map fig.3). He sold it to George Villiers, 1st. Duke of Buckingham. York Gate was built by the Duke's Master Mason, Nicholas Stone in 1626. It shows the line of the bank of the River Thames, before the building of the Embankment.

St. James'

In the fields west of the cross at Charing stood the hospital of St. James for lepers. It had been built during the reign of Henry III. Edward had granted the Hospital a fair in 1289 and Eleanor's executors paid it 6s. 8d. as a gift. Henry VIII built 'a goodly manor' on the requisitioned site 'annexing thereunto a park', serving St. James' and Whitehall.

PART XII

Westminster

The Royal Palace of Westminster

A residence at Westminster Abbey may have been built by Cnut. There is stronger evidence for a palace established there by Edward the Confessor. This is shown, in the Bayeux Tapestry, with round edged roof tiles, or shingles, windows, a towered entrance, an upper chamber, in which the bed, like that of Odysseus, appears to be supported by a tree post, penetrating through the floor from the hall below. The Confessor's bed is supplied with drapes. His seat in the hall is carved with animal heads, and with wall painting and hangings behind. Posts support the curved roof timbers.

The Great Hall of the Confessor's palace was rebuilt by William II 'Rufus' 1087-1099. Stow claims the new hall's dimensions were 240ft. x 74ft. This hall would have been the major part of the building described by Fitz-Stephen thus:-

'on the bank of the River the Royal Palace exalts its head and stretches wide, an incomparable structure, furnished with bastions and breast-work'.

It was likely to have been the hall in which the marriage of Edward I's Uncle Richard was celebrated in 1231, for which 30,000 dishes were ordered, and where, in 1241/2, Henry III feasted an 'innumerable multitude'.

The Liberate Rolls refer to the King's oriel window, (1236) the Queen's chapel, chamber and wardrobe (1237), and rushes from Kent for the floors of the Great and Lesser Halls (1245). In the grounds, offices (domestic) next to the hall, were to be removed and set up 'between the Exchequer and the gate', a chamber for the household knights built (1244), cherry trees planted in the King's garden (1239), and a vine-yard was established, it being William the Priest's task to hoop the wine barrels and carry out annual repairs (1269/70). Another component of the Palace was a chapel dedicated to St. Stephen, supposedly founded by King Stephen in the middle of the 12th. century.

The Palace Site

The 1290 palace grounds probably extended North of the present Bridge Street to adjoin the Archbishop of York's land, Westminster Bridge today replacing the old King's Bridge. On the East it was bounded by a wider River Thames. A quay is mentioned in the 13th. century rolls and there are several references to palace floods. St. Stephen's Chapel would have carried the Palace range southwards to the northern end of Abingdon Street. It is likely the Palace gardens and vine-yard lay at this southern end. The proximity of the Abbey Church on the West is demonstrated both in the Bayeux Tapestry, where the workman fixing the weather vane to the recently finished Abbey Church balances his ladder across the narrow gap, (*fig. 1*) and by the ease with which the fire of 1299 spread from the Palace to the Abbey. The Jewel Tower, built 1365 on land which had belonged to Westminster Abbey is just outside the Palace's South-west boundary.

1. The Confessor's Church

Palace Remains

The Palace not only suffered fire damage in 1299 but, according to Stow, 'a great part . . . . .was once again burnt in the year 1512, since which time it has not been re-edified. Only the Great Hall, with offices near adjoining, are kept in good reparation and serveth, as before, for feasts, coronations, arraignments, etc.' The only parts of the 1290 palace extant in situ are the lower walls of William II's Great Hall, now part of Westminster Hall. Capitals and a table end from this Hall may be seen in the Jewel Tower.

The Lesser Hall reputedly stood at the South end of the Great (Westminster) Hall, where the statue of Richard I on horseback is now situated, in the Old Palace Yard. This Lesser Hall may have been Stow's 'offices near adjoining'.

The crypt of St. Stephen's Chapel, which has survived, was furnished by Edward, as a chapel for his courtiers, but this had been done after Eleanor's death. The upper Chapel, re-built at least twice since Edward's time, was finally destroyed in the 1834 fire, and replaced by the present St. Stephen's Hall. Canons' Row recalls the canons who served St. Stephen's.

Westminster Abbey Church

An Early Church

Claims for a pre-Edward the Confessor church on Thorney Island, as the Abbey site was then called, are based on 8 suspect charters, legends told in the chronicles, and the discovery, in 1869 of a Romano-British sarcophagus and lid. The latter, bearing a carved cross, suggests a late 4th. century Christian burial. Provided the lid belonged to the sarcophagus and the burial had taken place either on the North Green, where the coffin was discovered, or within the vicinity, this would prove an early Christian settlement at Westminster. This sarcophagus and lid may be seen in the Undercroft at the present Abbey Church. Four articles on the subject were published in The Archaeological Association's Journal for 1870.

Legend claimed Sebert as the founder of an early church on the site, dedicated to St. Peter. A coffin believed to have contained his bones with those of his wife and his sister was incorporated into the 13th. century Abbey church. His tomb, constructed 1308, may be found in a recess in the South Ambulatory of the present church.

The Confessor's Church

The last years of Edward the Confessor's life were largely concerned with building or rebuilding a church next to his palace at Westminster. The Anglo-Saxon Chronicle gives the date of its consecration as December 28th. 1065, adding that the Confessor 'died on the eve of the 12th. day and was buried on the 12th. day in the same minster'.

The Bayeux Tapestry Representation (*see fig. 1*)

In the Tapestry, the Abbey church is correctly sited to the West of the Palace. The man positioning the weather-cock, possibly a device to indicate the church was 'new-built', appears to be balancing his ladder across the present St.

Margaret Street. The Tapestry presents the North side and transept of a cruciform building, with an off-central tower, surmounted by a dome, or an early Norman 'stunted' spire, and a cross. The Chancel, in keeping with the medieval practice, is hidden from public view, but the 'side off the dolls' house' technique, employed for buildings in the Tapestry, reveals a nave with piers and arches. The number - six - may be arbitary though Pevsner, on archaeological and documentary evidence, gives this church nave six double bays. A large arch supports the central tower. Although there is some disagreement over the interpretation of the Latin terms used in contemporary descriptions of this church (see Bond 'Westminster Abbey' 1909 pp.10 and 14) it is generally agreed that the Confessor's church had an apsidal east end and an unusually long nave. All that may now be seen of this Abbey church are the bases of three piers on either side of the High Altar in the Sanctuary of the present building.

Though built by a Saxon King, The Confessor's church is usually referred to as 'The Norman Church' as it was Norman in style.

Henry III's Abbey Church

In 1220, on the eve of his second coronation, the boy King, Henry III, laid the foundation stone of a Lady Chapel, to be built onto the East end of the Confessor's church. Although this chapel appears to have been nearing completion in 1240, when glass was ordered for the windows, work was resumed in 1245, for, by then, Henry III had decided to completely replace the Confessor's ageing church.

The first stage of Henry's re-building programme commenced in July 1246. The Court master mason at that time was a Henry de Reyns. His disappearance from the records 1253/4 coincides with the end of the first burst of building activity. He may have been related to Dymenge de Reyns (or Leger) who worked on the Queen's monuments.

During this period, four chapels were added to the eastern end, two each side of the Lady Chapel. The five chapels radiated from an ambulatory, which divided them from the Chancel, (that is St. Edward's Chapel, and the Sanctuary with the High Altar), and provided access for pilgrims. This brought the Abbey Church to the crossing, the North and South transepts. Wood for the Chancel roof and monks' stalls was ordered in 1252.

Outside the church, on the South side, a chapter house had been built. Matthew Paris commented on it in 1250. It was probably finished in 1253, and certainly in 1257 when Henry III held his Council there.

After Henry de Reyns, responsibility for the church devolved to John of Gloucester, who was ordered to demolish the Confessor's church 'next to the King's seat'. The transepts St. Faith's Chapel and first bay of the nave were raised by the end of John's term of office but it is not certain which of the two Master masons was responsible. If the carved mid-13th. century head of a master craftsman, to be found in the North transept, could be identified, it might illuminate the controversy.

A final building programme, carried out under Robert of Beverly from 1262 to 1269, drifted on until Henry III's death in November 1272. This took the nave to just beyond the fourth bay. The western extent of the 1290 church.

Apart from the Lady Chapel, which was destroyed for the present Henry VII Chapel, the fabric of Henry III's church, largely the 1290 church, has survived. The other four chapels may be found at the Eastern end of the present Abbey Church. Those on the North side were and are dedicated to St. John the Baptist and St. Paul.

St. John the Baptist

The vestibule to this chapel, known as Our Lady of the Pew, has been dated 14th. century by Pevsner. It may have been established by the widow of Aymer de Valence. There are no 13th. century monuments in this chapel, but 2 wall recesses have been dated 13th. century by Pevsner.

St. Paul

This chapel may have contained the cloth in which the head of St. Paul was reputedly wrapped after his execution. The earliest tomb here is post 1431. The monument to the Countess of Sussex has replaced the original altar.

The chapels on the south side of the Lady Chapel were and are dedicated to St. Nicholas and St. Edmund the King.

St. Nicholas

A finger of this patron saint of children was presented to the Abbey church by Eleanor herself. The earliest tomb is 15th. century.

St. Edmund the King

In this chapel may be found the tomb of William de Valence, half brother to Henry III who died in 1296. Both the reclining figure and the tomb chest are made of oak, covered with copper plates which were engraved and enamelled. Most of these have been lost from the chest.

The Tomb of the Royal Children

Just outside St. Edmund's Chapel, in the wall of the South Ambulatory, and towards the 14th. century chapel of St. Benedict, is the altar tomb of Edward's sister, Katherine, who died in 1257, aged 5. This tomb was originally decorated with mosaic, some of which remains. According to Bond ('Westminster Abbey p.180') four other children of Henry III and four children of Eleanor and Edward are buried in this tomb, supposedly removed from St. Edward's Chapel at the end of the 14th. century.

St. Edward's Chapel

This lies inside the Ambulatory of Henry III's church. Edward the Confessor had been buried before the altar of his Abbey church. St. Wulstan, Bishop of Worcester (1062-1095) raised a stone tomb over the King's remains. In 1102 this tomb had been opened in the presence of Henry I, revealing the 'perfectly preserved' body.

After the Confessor was canonised (1163) his body was transferred to a shrine in the presence of Henry II and Thomas Becket, the then newly appointed Archbishop of Canterbury. Henry III's plans for a new shrine to house his patron saint were afoot by November 8th. 1236, when he commanded Odo, the royal goldsmith, to make an image of the new Queen for the 'shrine of St. Edward' (Liberate Rolls). This was probably one of the 11 gold figures with which Henry's shrine was eventually furnished. Matthew Paris described the finished shrine as 'gold and of most precious workmanship' (Great Chronicle).

The Chapel, pedestal and shrine were eventually ready to receive the Saint. Peter of Rome had built this pedestal and laid the mosaic floor. *(see fig. 2)*. The translation took place on October 13th. 1269. The body was carried by Henry himself, his brother Richard and Richard's two sons, Henry of Almain and Edmund. Two years later Henry of Almain's heart was to be brought back (after his murder during mass at Viterbo) for burial in the same chapel.

The shrine disappeared at the Dissolution and the Saint's body was buried beneath the smashed pedestal. In 1554, under Mary, the pedestal was re-assembled and the body returned to the upper part. Although much of the decoration has gone, sufficient remains to show the pedestal was made of marble inlaid with glass mosaic and red Italian Porphyry.

By 1290 the Chapel had become a mausoleum for the royal family. J.C. Parsons (Eleanor of Castile's Birth and Children) gives evidence for the burials of five of Eleanor's children, Katherine, Joan, John, Henry and Alfonso, 'next the shrine of St. Edward'.

John and Margaret the children of Henry III's half-brother, William de Valence, were also buried there. Two slabs, in front of Henry V's chapel and largely covered, mark their graves. (Pevsner).

Henry III, who died in November 1272, is said to have been initially housed in St. Edward's vacated grave. Edward and Eleanor reputedly brought prophyry for his tomb back with them from Italy on their return from Acre. (Bond). The tomb image, the head probably based on that made for his funeral effigy which may be seen in the Undercroft Museum at the Abbey, was being made by William Torel at the same time as Eleanor's (1290-1292). Henry's tomb and image stand to the North of St. Edward's shrine.

It was here, too, that Eleanor was buried.

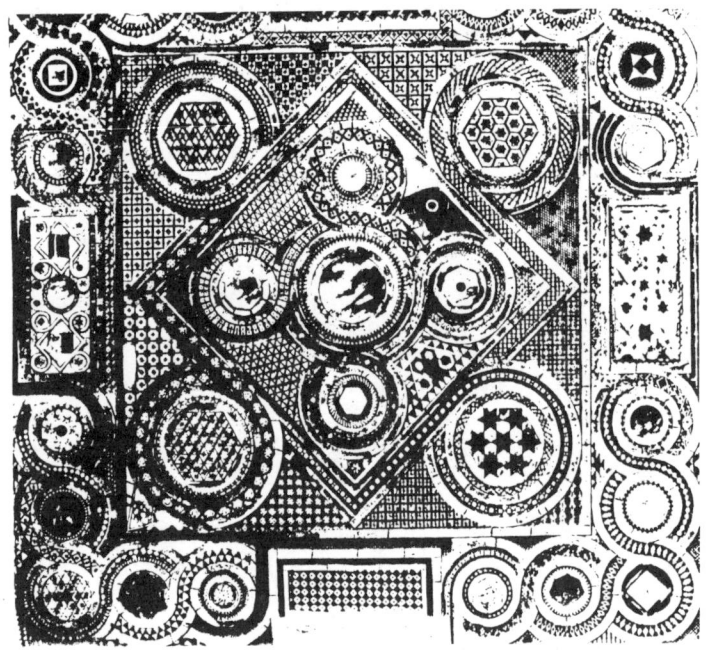

2. Mosaic Flooring

The Tomb of Eleanor of Castile

Eleanor's third and last tomb stands in St. Edward's Chapel, next to that of her father-in-law, Henry III. The materials for this tomb were amassed at Westminster during the Autumn and Winter of 1290. Stone was brought there by Galfrido the Chapman (trader). Metal for all three tomb images was bought from William Sprot and John Ware, beaters, of London. £25. 16s. 6d. was paid to Hugo Megge for wax which was carried from London.

This tomb image, which has survived, was made by William Torel, later in the accounts of the Queen's executors, described as a gold-smith. An initial payment is recorded on October 28th. 1290, a month before the Queen's death. Torels held the manor of Thurrock, Essex (Patent Roll 1289). Eleanor had been there on July 5th. 1290 and was joined by Edward on July 6th. ('The Court and Household of Eleanor of Castile in 1290' J.C. Parsons) so it is possible the work had been commissioned prior to her death, as the heart chapel at Black Friars had been.

Torel was paid a total of £33. 13s. 4d. for the joint images of Henry III and Queen Eleanor and £66. 6s. 8d. for work on the Queen's alone. The last payment for the Queen's image was recorded between Easter and Whitsun 1292. The gold coins for gilding had been bought the previous Autumn, and scaffolding for lifting the image into position, barriers around the tomb and a canopy above, probably all of wood, had been paid for just before January 31st. 1292, suggesting the Queen's image was finished, and in situ, before Torel's last payment.

The large quantities of wax and relative amounts of metal bought for the images in the accounts suggest solid images were made by the following process. Figures carved from wax would be coated with clay, leaving exits. The whole would be baked, when the melted wax would run out of the exits and probably be collected for other usage. The cooled clay shell could then be placed upright in a pit, pipes introduced through the exit holes to allow the escape of air, earth and rubble placed around it for support, and the molten metal poured into the space which had been occupied by the wax.

When the metal was set, the whole could be lifted from the pit with the aid of hoists (scaffolding), the outer clay shell removed, and the image cleaned and polished.

Each image of the Queen, being separately carved, would be slightly different, which is suggested by the remaining evidence of the surviving image at Westminster and the drawing of that at Lincoln.

The image on the Westminster tomb, and possibly the others as well, was gilded. During the Autumn of 1291 the executors made three purchases of florins, gold coins first minted by the Florentines, supposed to weigh 54 grains (9/80ths of an ounce) each. In all, 544 florins were bought at a cost of £67. 19s. 8d. There was a 2.8oz. discrepancy between the mark weight of 64 oz. and the official florin weight of 61.2oz. (544 x 9/80 oz.)

The wooden barriers, required as a temporary measure to protect the tomb from pilgrims and the sick who visited St. Edward's tomb, had been made, as had the scaffolding and canopy, by Thomas of Hoctune, a carpenter, later described as an engineer. They were replaced with metalwork made by Thomas of Leghtone (possibly of Leighton Buzzard) a smith, for an agreed sum of £12. Thomas actually received £13, the extra £1 being for the carriage of the ironwork from Leghtone to Westminster, setting it up in position, and the payment of his man. Leyton's metalwork grill may still be seen from the ambulatory. (*see fig. 3*).

After January 31st.1292, Walter of Dunolmia was employed to decorate 'all over' the tombs of Henry and Eleanor. A fragment of his painting by Eleanor's tomb has survived, and a reconstruction may be seen in the North ambulatory. More paintings of the same period, and probably by the same artist, have survived on the South wall of the South transept by St. Faith's chapel. One showing St. Christopher and the other 'doubting Thomas'.

3. Thomas Leghtone's Grill

The Sanctuary

West of St. Edward's Chapel lie the High Altar and the Sanctuary. As in St. Edward's Chapel, the floor of the Sanctuary had been paved by decorators belonging to the

Cosmati of Rome, brought over by Abbot Ware. Here the work, executed under Odoricus, was more elaborate.

Eleanor's sister-in-law, Aveline de Forz, the first wife of Edward's younger brother Edmund 'Crouchback', had been buried in the Sanctuary (1273). In 1296, Edmund himself was buried here, and in 1324, Aymer de Valence, the son of William. Aymer was with Edward when he died in 1307 at Burgh on Sands. Abbot Ware and Walter Wenlock, who was Abbot of Westminster in 1290, also lie in the Sanctuary.

Eleanor's Final Burial

It is likely Eleanor was brought to the Abbey Church on Saturday December 16th., and her coffin 'full of spices' laid before the High Altar. The reredos was raised c. 1400 so, in 1290, the Sanctuary and St. Edward's Chapel were not so divided. The Benedictine monks from the Abbey could have kept the Vigil.

The 13th. Century Monastery

Remnants of the early monastic buildings may be found South of Henry III's Chapter House, which had been built on part of the monks' graveyard. At the South end of the East Cloister is the undercroft of the 'Norman' monastery. It is now divided into two, identified as 'The Pyx Chamber and Treasury' and 'The Undercroft Museum'. Between the Pyx Chamber and the entrance to the Chapter House is a stairway, leading to the present Library, part of the Monks' Dormitory, which once lay above the whole undercroft. These Day Stairs gave the monks access from their dormitory to the cloister. Their night stairs, leading from the dormitory into the Abbey Church, crossed the passage entrance to the Chapter House.

South-east of the undercroft lay the infirmary block. The infirmary itself was where the Little Cloister is now situated. St. Catherine's, the infirmary chapel may be seen at the eastern end.

The Hearse

In the accounts of the Queen's executors, Robert de Colebroke was paid £3.15s.2d. for making the 'herses' at Black Friars and at Westminster. A herse was either a temporary monument raised over a grave, or a carriage on which the body is carried to the grave. As the latter had been in use during the journey of the Cortège, and as herses were required at both burials, it may be assumed Robert was to construct the latter.

In 'Ceremonies and Services at Court in the Time of Henry VII' the following instructions are given for making

a royal herse. 'There must be made a herse rail and the bars and the (back) ground clothed with black and there must be timber upon the same herse for to bear the light of wax and also branches of timber to bear the morteys (?) of wax wt. lights and 13 principal buttress tapirs (candles tapering at the top) and as many course (corpse?) lights.'
Eleanor's 'herse' would have been out of commission by 1292 when the tomb was finished.

The Service

As a quarrel was in progress between the Abbot, Walter Wenlock, and the Archbishop of Canterbury, John Peckham, the funeral service was conducted by Oliver Sutton, Bishop of Lincoln. He is likely to have accompanied the Cortège from Lincoln. Eleanor's final funeral took place on Sunday December 17th. 1290.

Edward's Death and Tomb

There are some similarities between the deaths of Edward and Eleanor. At least from May 1306, when he was carried in a litter to the 'Feast of Swans', Edward had been ill. Like Eleanor he was on the road to within a few days of his death and died at a remote settlement - not Harby, but Burgh by Sands, c. 6 miles North-west of Carlisle (July 7th. 1307). His body, too, was brought to Waltham Abbey, the Priory of the Holy Trinity and St. Edward's Chapel, Westminster Abbey Church. Edward was buried on the other (West) side of his father, Henry III.

Unlike Eleanor's, Edward's tomb is undecorated and there is no tomb image. This was probably because of Edward's instructions to his son, Edward II, that, 'as often as the Scots rebel' he should 'assemble the people against them and carry with him the bones of his father'. (Froissart). Though the grisly instructions were not implemented, the body was kept in seeming readiness, wax cloths for it being provided until the deposition of Richard II (1399), so that this tomb fulfilled the function of a storage chest, rather than that of a memorial.

The Queen's Anniversary

Edward gave properties from Eleanor's estate, the income from which was to finance prayers, services, and gifts of money and food made to the poor, for the 'health of her soul'. The most substantial of these was made to Westminster Abbey. So many manors were involved that the Abbey appointed a special officer to be in charge of 'Queen Eleanor's Manors'.

The Charter confirming the gift and duties was signed by Edward at Berwick on Tweed on October 20th. 1291. At the Abbey the ceremony was to be directed by the Abbot, or, if he were absent, by the Prior or some other eminent prelate; to involve the whole convent, and to take place on St. Andrew's Eve, (6 p.m. November 28th. to 6 p.m. November 29th.) - the anniversary of the Queen's death. The King's Charter was to be read to the assembled convent, in the Chapter House. One hundred wax candles, each weighing 12 lbs. were to be lit about the Queen's tomb. In present day wax this would give candles 4 inches in diameter and 30 inches high.

The ceremony was to open with the singing of the Placebo, (vespers for the dead) and 'Lead me O Lord' (Psalm 5 v. 8) known as the Dirige. This would probably take place at the hour of Vespers i.e. 6 p.m. The whole was to conclude the following day with Mass sung at the High Altar, masses and prayers said by individual members of the Convent for the souls of Eleanor and all the faithful, accompanied by the ringing of bells, both great and small. The 100 candles were then to be extinguished, to be re-lit on special occasions through out the year and re-placed at the following anniversary. Two smaller candles of 2 lbs. each were to be kept burning continuously at Eleanor's tomb.

Alms of one penny sterling were then to be given and dole to 140 people.

Epilogue

After the funeral Edward left Westminster, by way of London and Enfield, for Ashridge, Buckinghamshire. Here, by 1285, Edward's cousin Edmund, the son of Uncle Richard, had founded a college for a Rector and about 20 canons, known as bon-hommes. This convent, of either friars or mystics, was, according to Tanner, surrounded by a park five miles in diameter, and would have provided an ideal retreat for Edward. He stayed there for five weeks much to the annoyance of the Cellarer of Dunstable who had to victual the Court! (Annuls of Dunstable).

On January 3rd. he wrote to the Abbot of Cluny, requesting this Benedictine monastery to pray for 'our consort whom in life we loved dearly and dead we do not cease to love.' (Foedera).

The Chronicler of St. Alban's wrote Eleanor's valediction.

'She was the pillar of all England. . . Like the Dawn she struck with her rod of brightness and drove away the darkness of our night'.

DATE	OVERNIGHT STOPPING PLACE	ADDITIONAL DETAIL [AND EVIDENCE]	APPROX DISTANCE (MILES)
Tue Nov 28	Harby	Eleanor dies at the house of Richard Weston between 6pm and midnight [Household Accounts]	-
Wed Nov 29 to Sat Dec 2	Lincoln	The body is brought to Lincoln and embalmed [Writ/Accounts]	16 or 9½
Sun Dec 3	Lincoln	Burial of viscera at the Cathedral [Tomb]	
Mon Dec 4	Grantham	Queen at St Wulfram's Court at the Castle or Angel [Cross]	26
Tue Dec 5	Stamford	Castle and/or Friary [Writ signed at Great Casterton on Dec 5; Cross]	22
Wed Dec 6	Stamford or Geddington	Royal Palace at Geddington [Cross] and	19
Thur Dec 7	Geddington or Northampton	Church of St Mary Magdalene	28
Fri Dec 8	Northampton	Castle and St Andrew's Priory [Writ, Dec 9; Cross]	
Sat Dec 9	Stony Stratford	Bradwell Abbey (?) [Cross]. The King had probably left the cortège	14
Sun Dec 10	Woburn	Abbey (Toddington?) [Cross]	16
Mon Dec 11	Dunstable	Priory. The King not recorded as present at the selection of the cross site [Chronicle; Cross]	9
Tue Dec 12	St Albans	Abbey. The King rejoins the cortège [Chronicle; Writ of Dec 13; Cross]	15
Wed Dec 13	Waltham	Abbey [Cross]	25
Thu Dec 14	London	Pass through the Priory of the Holy Trinity. Select cross site in West Cheap [Writ of Dec 14]	
Fri Dec 15	London	Second burial (heart) at Blackfriars [Writ of Dec 15; Accounts]	17
Sat Dec 16	Westminster	via Charing [Cross] to the Palace	1½
Sun Dec 17	Westminster	Third and final funeral at the Abbey [Tomb]	
TOTAL		12 journeys	208½ maximum

4. Summary of the Journey

ILLUSTRATIONS and MAPS

COVER
    Eleanor and Edward - Lincoln Cathedral photo by Paul Moorhouse.

PART I
1. Family Trees
2. Basingwerk Monastery, Flintshire
3. Rhuddlan Castle
4. Acton Burnell Castle Ruins
5. The Northern Tour
6. The Ruins of the Royal Hunting Lodge, Clipstone
7. Harby Church
8. The Site of Richard Weston's House

PART II
1. The Journey to Westminster - route map drawn by Dr. W. Powrie
2. 3 Ways to Lincoln
3. A Reaper's cart going up hill
4. Speed's Map
5. Newport Arch
6. Plan of Lincoln Castle
7. Building a Motte from the Bayeux Tapestry
8. Lucy Tower at Lincoln Castle
9. Pottergate
10. The Bishop's Palace
11. St. Mary's Gildhall
12. The Queen's Seal
13. The Image from the Re-created Tomb
14. The Cross Site
15. Fragment of the Lincoln Cross

PART III
1. The Castle Door
2. The 'Angel' Gate
3. The Market Cross

PART IV
1. Speed's Map
2. The Castle Ruins
3. Wall Bastion
4. Stukeley's Gate and Garden
5. The Franciscan Friary Gate - Arms of Henry Foyer
6. St. Leonard's Priory
7. The River Welland - dividing for the King's Mill and the Abbot's Mill

PART V
1. The King's Door and pier with volute and waterleaf capital. Photo by the Rev. Richard Dorrington.
2. Geddington Cross - drawing by Jill Sturman
3. Cross - detail of stonework with Church behind. Photo by the Rev. Richard Dorrington.

PART VI
1. The 13th. century Bridge over the River Ise at Geddington.
2. Speed's Map
3. The Castle Ruins from 'The Gentleman's Magazine' October 1800
4. The Northampton Cross drawing by Jill Sturman

PART VII
1. Partly demolished Priory Church at Dunstable
2. Reconstruction of the Church
3. and of the Priory drawn by F.A. Fowler

PART VIII
1. The River Ver at the 'Fighting Cocks'
2. Speed's Pictorial Plan of 'Verolanium' and St. Alban's
3. Aerial view of St. Alban's Cathedral and Abbey Church
4. The Cross Site

PART IX
1. Waltham Abbey Church showing 'Harold's Grave'
2. Waltham Cross with the Falcon Inn, the Four Swans and the Victorian Railings after the 1889 Restoration
3. Norman Arches Waltham Abbey Church

PART X
1. Edward Entering London
2. Aldgate c.1759
3. The East End of Old St. Paul's showing St. Faith's Crypt
4. Fragments from the Cheapside Cross in the Museum of London
5. The Destruction of Cheapside Cross

PART XI
1. London - showing Ludgate, the Black Friary and church Old St. Paul's and the Tower
2. London c. 1300
3. Ralph Aggas' Map
4. Durham House by Antonie van den Wyngaerde
5. Charing Cross - a reconstruction based on the drawing now in the Crowle collection at the British Museum

PART XII
1. The Confessor's Church
2. Mosaic Flooring
3. Thomas Leghtone's Grill
4. Summary of the Journey

A BASIC BIBLIOGRAPHY

ABEL John (Ed.) Memorials of Queen Eleanor (1864)... reprinted by Cromwell Press 1990.
BEDE   A History of the English Church and People translated by Leo Sherley-Price....Penguin Classics 1977.
BENHAM Canon and WELCH Charles
    Medieval London.... The MacMillan Co.1901.
BLATCH M.   A Guide to London's Churches... Constable 1978.
BOND F.   Dedications and Patron Saints of English Churches... O.U.P. 1914.
BOND F.   Westminster Abbey... O.U.P. 1909.
BOOK OF KNIGHTS' FEES   H.M.S.O.
BRIDGES   The History and Antiquities of Northamptonshire... Whalley, Oxford 1791.
BRITISH ARCHAEOLOGICAL ASSOCIATION   Journals.
BUND (Ed.)   The Register of Bishop Godfrey Giffard 1268-1301/2 Worcestershire Historical Society... James Parker & Co. Oxford 1902.
BYERLY B.F. and C.R. (Ed.)
    Records of the Wardrobe and Household 1285-6, and 1286-9.... London H.M.S.O. 1977 and 1986.
CALENDARS OF ROLLS
    Chancery, Charter, Close, Inquisitions Miscellaneous and Post Mortem, Liberate, Patent, Published for H.M.S.O. by Eyre and Spottiswood.
CAMDEN W.   Britannia translated etc. by Edmund Gibson..... London 1695.
CANDIDUS Hugh   see MELLOWS
CARPENTER E. A House of Kings....John Baker London 1966.
COX J. Charles   Lincolnshire.....Methuen 1916.
DEFOE Daniel.   Tour through the Whole Island of Great Britain.... Dent 1927.
DOUBLEDAY J. Arthur (Ed. see also PAGE)
    The Victoria History of the Counties of England.... Dawson of Pall Mall.
    Bedfordshire 1972, Buckingham 1969, Hertfordshire 1971, Northampton 1970.
DOUGLAS (Ed.)   English Historical Documents....Eyre and Spottiswoode 1953.
DUGDALE William   Baronage of England... Thomas Newcomb 1676.
DUGDALE William   Monasticon Anglicanum... Longman, Hurst etc. 1817.
DUGDALE William   The Antiquities of Warwickshire... re-printed by John Jones 1765.

FERNIE E.C. The Romanesque Church of Waltham Abbey from the Journal of the British Archaeological Ass. Vol. CXXXVIII 1985.
FIENNES (see MORRIS)
FITZSTEPHEN (see SPARKE and WHEATLEY)
FLORENCE OF WORCESTER A History of the Kings of England translated by Joseph Stephenson in 1853..... re-printed Llanerch Enterprises, Dyfed.
FOWLER F.A. Dunstable Priory Church, a brief History and Guide ... The Church District Council.
FROISSART Jean Chronicles translated by John Bourchier, Lord Berners (1467-1534)...re-printed Harrap 1912.
FURTADO Peter, etc. (Ed.) Guide to Castles in Britain... O.S. Hamlyn.
GERALD OF WALES The Journey through Wales/The Description of Wales translated by Lewis Thorpe. . . Penguin Classics 1984.
GROSE and ASTLE Antiquarian Repertory...Edward Jeffery 1808.
GUISBOROUGH (see ROTHWELL)
HALLIWELL J. (Ed.) The Chronicle of William de Rishanger Camden Society...John Bowyer Nichols and Son 1840.
HARVEY John English Medieval Architects....Batsford 1954.
HEARNE Thomas Chronica Anglia....Oxford 1709.
HEARNE Thomas (Ed.) The Itineraries of John Leland 2nd. edition. Oxford 1745.
HILL Sir F. Medieval Lincoln....C.U.P. 1948.
HINDLE B.P. Medieval Roads....Shire Archaeology 1982.
HONEYBONE M. The Book of Grantham... Barracuda Books Ltd. 1980.
HUNTER J. On the Death of Eleanor of Castile in Archaeologia 29 (pp.167-191) 1842.
INGRAM The Rev. J. Translated 1823. The Anglo-Saxon Chronicle Everyman....Dent.
JUSSERLAND (translated by Lucy Toulmin Smith) English Wayfaring Life in the Middle Ages... T. Fisher Unwin 1899.
LAWRENCE C.H. Medieval Monasticism (2nd edition)...Longman 1989.
LEACH T. (Ed.) A Swinethorpe and Harby Miscellany...published by the author 1988.
LINGARD J. A History of England...Mawman, London 1825.
LUARD H.R.(Ed.) Annales Monastici (A.D. 1-1432) Rolls Series No. 36 Vols 3 (Dunstable) and 4 (Osney)...London 1864-9. Chronica Majora (Matthew Paris) Rolls series No. 57...London 1872-83. Flores Historiarum (Matthew of Westminster) Rolls series No.95...London 1890.
MARGARY I. Roman Roads in Britain...Phoenix House Ltd. London 1955.
MELLOWS W. (Ed.) The Peterborough Chronicle of Hugh Candidas ....London 1949.
MORRIS C. (Ed.) Celia Fiennes' Journey...Cresset Library 1947.
MORRIS J. (Ed.) Domesday Book in the History from the Sources series.... Phillimore.
20 Bedfordshire 1977, 13 Buckinghamshire 1978, 12 Hertfordshire 1976, 31 Lincolnshire 1986, 21 Northamptonshire 1979, 28 Nottinghamshire 1977, 29 Rutland 1980.

MORTON H.V.	A Stranger in Spain. . . .Methuen 1955.
MYERS J.	The English Settlements in The Oxford History of England. . . .Clarendon 1986.
PAGE W. (Ed.)	The Victoria History of the Counties of England. Lincolnshire. . . .Constable 1906 Nottinghamshire. . . .Constable 1906
PARSONS J.C.	The Court and Household of Eleanor of Castile in 1290 (1984).
PARSONS J.C.	The Year of Eleanor of Castile's Birth and her Children by Edward I in Medieval Studies No.46 (1984) Pontifical Institute of Medieval Studies, Toronto.
PARSONS J.C.	Eleanor of Castile and the Viscountess Jeanne of Chatelleraut in Genealogist' Magazine Vo. XXIII No. 4 (Dec. 1989)
PERCY T. (Ed.)	Reliques of Ancient English Poetry Vol. 2. . .Dent.
PEVSNER N.	The Buildings of England series. . .Penguin Books. Bedfordshire etc. 1968, Buckinghamshire 1973, Hertfordshire revised by B. Cherry 1978, Lincolnshire with J. Harris revised by N. Antrim 1989, Northamptonshire revised by B. Cherry 1973, Nottinghamshire revised by E. Williamson 1979.
PIGGOT S.	William Stukeley revised and enlarged edition Thames & Hudson 1985.
PINCHES J.H. & R.V.	Royal Heraldry of England. . .Heraldry Today 1974.
POWICKE Sir M.	The 13th Century The Oxford History of England. . . Clarendon 1985.
RENN D.F.	Norman Castles in Britain. . .Baker 1968.
RILEY H.T. (Ed.)	Chronica Monasterii S. Albani (A.D. 793-1488) Rolls Series 28. . . .London 1863-76.
RIMMER A.	Ancient Stone Crosses of England. . .Virtue, Spalding & Co. 1875.
ROLLS	(see Calendars)
ROTHWELL H. (Ed.)	The Chronicle of Walter of Guisborough. Camden, London 1957.
RYMER T.	Foedera etc. . . .A. & J. Churchill 1710.
SALMON J.	Acton Burneel and its Church. . .Redverse Ltd. 1974.
SPARKE J. (Ed.)	Fitzstephen's Life of Becket in Historiae Anglicanae . . . .London 1723.
STOW	see WHEATLEY
STREET The Rev. B.	Historical Notes on Grantham & Grantham Church. . . .Ridge & Son 1857.
STRICKLAND A.	Lives of the Queens of England. . . Cedric Chivers Ltd. Bath 1972.
STUKELEY W.	Diaries and Letters. . .The Surtees Society 1883.
TANNER L.	Unknown Westminster Abbey. . . Penguin Books 1948.
TANNER T.	Notita Monastica. . . .C.U.P. 1787.
TURNER T.H. (Ed.)	Manners and Household Expenses of England in the 13th and 15th Centuries (Roxburghe Club). . . William Nicol Shakespeare Press 1841.
WALTER OF GUISBOROUGH see ROTHWELL.	
WALSINGHAM see RILEY.	
WHEATLEY H.B. (Ed.)	John Stow A Survey of London including Fitzstephen's Description of London in Everyman Classics series. . . .Dent 1987.
WILFORD J.	Beneath the Stonebow Centre. . . .Flare 1983.

WINSTON R.   Becket. . . .Constable, London 1967.
WINSTON T.   The Priory Church of St. Bartholomew the Great. . . reprinted 1985.
YOUNG E. & W.   London's Churches. . . Grafton Books 1986.

MAPS

20th Century
A.A.   The Book of London.
A–Z   Lincoln, London, Northampton.
O.S.   (in route order) Lincoln Landranger 121, Lincoln and Grantham 1920 revised 1947 113, Grantham and surrounding area Landranger 130, Kettering, Corby and surrounding area Landranger 141, Northampton and Milton Keynes area Landragner 152, Luton, Hertford and surrounding area Landranger 166.

Early Maps
BLAEU   Atlas of England, Scotland, Wales and Ireland, facsimile of maps published 1645 & 1654. . .Thames & Hudson, London.
SAXTON C.   Atlas of England and Wales 1579; facsimiles published by The British Library 1963-83.
SPEED J.   England; facsimile of the 1st. edition of 1611. . . . Phoenix House Ltd. Charing Cross 1953.
STOW J.   Map of London (see Wheatley)

Contours
The Royal Road Book of England . . . . Gall & Inglis, London and Edinburgh 1918.

ELEANOR'S COATS OF ARMS

England

Castile and Leon

Ponthieu